Missing in Modern Bibles

The Old Heresy Revived

AV Seminar Studies

Jack Moorman

REL006201: Religion: Biblical Studies - Topical

ISBN 978-0-9822230-4-8

All Scripture quotes are from the King James Bible except those verses compared and then the source is identified.

Address All Inquiries To:
THE DEAN BURGON SOCIETY
OR
THE BIBLE FOR TODAY
900 Park Avenue
Collingswood, New Jersey 08108
BFT #3426

Web: www.biblefortoday.org
E-mail: bft@biblefortoday.org

Formatted and Indexed by Dr. H. D. Williams, M.D., Ph.D.
THE OLD PATHS PUBLICATIONS, Inc.
142 Gold Flume Way
Cleveland, Georgia, U.S.A.

Web: www.theoldpathspublications.com
E-mail: TOP@theoldpathspublications.com

1.0

DEDICATION

It is with thankfulness to God that I dedicate this book to H.R. (Randy) Pike now living in Greenville S.C. Though now in frail health: a powerful preacher, faithful missionary, and choice servant of Jesus Christ, who in 1970 at a hotel in Johannesburg, South Africa, introduced me to the Defence of the Received Text and Authorised Version.

Jack Moorman

"Heaven and earth shall pass away, but my words shall not pass away." (Matthew 24:35)

TABLE OF CONTENTS

"But he answered and said, It is written, Man shall not live by bread alone, but by every word that proceedeth out of the mouth of God." (Matthew 4:4)

INTRODUCTION

Would it make a difference if you knew that the New Testament of your Modern Bible did not have First and Second Peter? Yet if the total number of missing words were added up this is how much shorter the modern translations are than the King James Version. Is it a cause for concern if in over 175 instances the names of Christ are missing, or if the word "hell" is not found in the Old Testament, or if key doctrinal passages have been diminished? And, the biggest shock of all! Is it possible that the most basic and blatant of all early heresies concerning the Person of Christ has been given a new lease on life in the modern Bibles? That these things are so, with the reasons why, are set forth in the following pages.

Many have gone over to the new Bibles without realising that much more is involved than the question of modern English. The entire fabric has been affected! The underlying text is substantially different. The philosophy and methodology of the translators is in marked contrast to that of the Authorised Version. The English of the new versions is assumed at first to be easier, but whether it is actually more readable, authoritative, and conducive to meditation, study, and memorization is another matter.

From 1611 until our generation there was only one widely used Bible in the English-speaking world. The AV became the Standard in that empire upon which the sun never set, and in that language which is the primary vehicle of international discourse. It penetrated the world's continents and brought multitudes to saving faith in Christ. It became the impetus of the great missionary movements. Through it, Christian workers heard and answered the call to world evangelisation. It was the source of the greatest revivals since the days of the Apostles. Street preachers, colporteurs, church planters, Sunday school teachers, and tract distributors took the King James Bible into teeming cities and across country lanes. It was the high water mark in the history of the Gospel's spread.

However, in this world there is always an onslaught against truth and righteousness, and a tendency to put aside the good and substitute something that is inferior. And so, during the Nineteenth Century the call for a revised Bible began to be heard. For the most part and certainly in the beginning the call did not come from fervent Bible believers, but rather those who were leaning toward theological liberalism. It came from men who were comfortable with the rising tide of rationalism, Darwin, and the back-to-Rome movement.

The first major revision was published in 1881. After the initial excitement there was little public support. The same lack of acceptance greeted the American (ASV) edition in 1901. Others followed: Weymouth, Williams, Moffat, Beck, Goodspeed, Twentieth Century, but still with little impact. But in 1952 came the Revised Standard Version, produced with the backing of the liberal National Council of Churches in the U.S.A. The pace now quickened; public acceptance began to rise. Others followed: The New English, Amplified, Berkley, Phillips, Wuest, Living, New American, Good News, Jerusalem, and especially the New International. Each came with the promise that they were based on the earliest manuscripts and the latest scholarship, and that God's Word would now be more easily understood.

Taking up this last point, it is interesting to see the names given to a number of these versions: The Authentic New Testament, The N.T. in Plain English, the N.T. in Basic English, The Simplified N.T. in Plain English for Today's Reader, Inspired Letters of the N.T. in Clearest English! And then a number of the revisions have been revised: The New Revised Standard Version, the New Berkley Version, The New (that's right!) Jerusalem Bible. Recently a (New) NIV has been announced. There have been upwards of one hundred modern Bibles published in the English language.

After one hundred attempts to replace the Authorised Version, one cannot help wonder whether God wants it replaced! This conviction is strengthened when we note that believers do not study the modern versions as they once did the AV. They are not marked up and study worn. Passages are seldom memorized. Preachers do not quote verses from the NIV in the pulpit as they once did the AV. The same is true of Sunday school memorization. Nor is expository preaching and doctrinal study emphasized as it once was. What is more, the issue of authority has been undermined. "What does the Bible say," has been replaced by an anaemic, "How does this version render the passage." And then, is it a coincidence that this multiplication of versions comes at the same time as the tongues, prophecies, and extra-biblical revelations of the charismatic movement? Thus, it may be rightly asked, where are we to go to hear God's Word today?

The AV English is said to be difficult to understand. Indeed, it is *different*. It is not like your morning newspaper; but its English is not difficult, as a section-by-section comparison with other translations will show. For a computer generated analysis of this question see *The Reading Ease of the King James Bible* by D. A. Waite Jr. Using four readability formulas, (Flesch Reading Ease, Flesch Grade Level, Flesch-Kincaid, Gunning Fog Index), Mr. Waite's research shows the AV to be rated as "fairly easy." Though 400 years old, on the question of *readability alone*, the AV achieved approximately the same scores as five recent versions. He also shows that AV words are frequently shorter in syllables and letters.

In other respects, there is no comparison. A section-by-section comparison will show that while the AV is a *formal* equivalence translation (word for word from the original) rather than the so-called *dynamic* equivalence, its English has depths and fountains. It is living and rhythmic. In contrast, the English of modern versions has been shown to be "Formica flat," tepid, wooden. Recent authors, often secular, have stressed this point. The AV can be read aloud, memorized, and quoted with authority and reverence. It has rhythm. It flows. By comparison, in public reading, we do not have this cadence and timing in the NIV, NASV and NKJV. They are broken and disjointed, with halts and breaks.

Modern Bibles are not *held dear* as the AV was. The following quotation from Psalm 23:1 of the *Contemporary English Version* gives and indication as to why this is.

> You, Lord are my shepherd, I will never be in need. You let
> me rest in fields of green grass.

The AV displays the full flowering of the English language, and in fact shaped that language. It is not archaic or Elizabethan, as comparison with that era will show. It was never contemporary, but always a step apart from the common.

The great "problem" with understanding the Bible is the fact that *it is* the Bible! It cannot be read like other books. Unless the Author is known by personal faith in Jesus Christ, or in the case of a lost person, by the convicting work of the Holy Spirit, it will not be understood or appreciated. No amount of translational skill or modern English idiom can cross that gap. It must be read with a submissive heart to God.

The following is intended to show that whatever help a modern version may claim to give; the price paid in missing words, lack of reverence, doctrinal weakening, lessened readability, and (!) the reintroduction of an ancient heresy, is simply too great.

The modern Bibles have several basic characteristics. What is said about one can usually be said about another. As the New International Version is the current bestseller we will use it as a representative of the others in comparisons with the King James Version.

This study, which is being used in Bible Version seminars in Great Britain, is a substantially enlarged revision of the author's previous *Missing in Modern Bibles* and *Modern Bibles – The Dark Secret*.

Jack Moorman
London, England
2009

1 Peter 1:23-25 Being born again, not of corruptible seed, but of incorruptible, by the word of God, which liveth and abideth for ever. For all flesh is as grass, and all the glory of man as the flower of grass. The grass withereth, and the flower thereof falleth away: But the word of the Lord endureth for ever. And this is the word which by the gospel is preached unto you.

CHAPTER 1

Key Passages Missing

The first list is a partial sampling of the kind of words and phrases that are missing from the Modern Bibles. These omissions often diminish the basic doctrines. The New International Version, which we have used as our representative, has somewhat fewer omissions than the New American Standard, Revised Standard, New English, and Good News Bible etc. But they are, nevertheless, considerable. This will become increasingly evident when we look at the second list that gives the Names of Deity that have been omitted. From the Gospel of Matthew the two translations placed together, this will enable you can come to a conclusion as to whether the NIV has the same sense of authority, reverence, and readability as the KJV.

The first passage in each example is from the KJV:

Matthew 1:25
- And knew her not till she had brought forth her <u>firstborn</u> son.
- But he had no union with her until she gave birth to a son.

Matthew 5:44
- But I say unto you, Love your enemies, <u>bless them that curse you, do good to them that hate you,</u> and pray for them which despitefully use you, and persecute you.
- But I tell you; Love your enemies and pray for those who persecute you.

Matthew 6:13
- And lead us not into temptation, but deliver us from evil: <u>For thine is the kingdom, and the power and the glory, forever. Amen.</u>
- And lead us not into temptation, but deliver us from the evil one.

Matthew 9:13
- For I am not come to call the righteous, but sinners <u>to repentance.</u>
- For I have not come to call the righteous but sinners.

Matthew 15:8
- This people <u>draweth nigh unto me with their mouth,</u> and honoureth me with their lips; but their heart is far from me.
- These people honour me with their lips, but their hearts are far from me.

Matthew 16:3
- <u>O ye hypocrites,</u> ye can discern the face of the sky, but can ye not discern the signs of the times?

- You know how to interpret the appearance of the sky, but you cannot interpret the signs of the times.

Matthew 17:21

- Howbeit this kind goeth not out but by prayer and fasting.
- Missing in NIV.

Matthew 19:9

- And I say unto you, Whosoever shall put away his wife except it be for fornication, and shall marry another, committeth adultery: and whoso marrieth her which is put away doth commit adultery.
- I tell you that anyone who divorces his wife, except for marital unfaithfulness and marries another woman commits adultery.

Matthew 20:16

- So the last shall be first and the first last: for many be called but few chosen.
- So the last will be first, and the first will be last.

Matthew 20:22

- But Jesus answered and said, Ye know not what ye ask. Are ye able to drink of the cup that I shall drink of, and to be baptized with the baptism that I am baptized with?
- Ye don't know what you are asking, Jesus said to them. Can you drink the cup I am going to drink?

Matthew 23:14

- Woe unto you, scribes and Pharisees, hypocrites! for ye devour widows' houses, and for a pretence make long prayer: therefore ye shall receive the greater damnation.
- Missing in NIV.

Matthew 27:35

- And they crucified him, and parted his garments, casting lots: that it might be fulfilled which was spoken by the prophet, They parted my garments among them, and upon my vesture did they cast lots.
- When they had crucified him, they divided up his clothes by casting lots.

Hereafter, only the missing phrases are shown:

Mark

- 1:14 Jesus came into Galilee, preaching the gospel of the kingdom of God.
- 1:31 and immediately the fever left her.
- 2:17 I came not to call the righteous, but sinners to repentance.
- 6:11 Verily I say unto you, It shall be more tolerable for Sodom and Gomorrah in the day of judgment than for that city.

- 7:8   Ye hold the tradition of men, <u>as the washing of pots and cups: and many other   such like things ye do.</u>
- 7:16   <u>If any man have ears to hear, let him hear.</u>
- 9:44   <u>Where their worm dieth not, and the fire is not quenched.</u>
- 9:46   <u>Where their worm dieth not, and the fire is not quenched.</u>
- 9:49   For every one shall be salted with fire <u>and every sacrifice shall be salted with salt.</u>
- 10:21 come, <u>take up the cross,</u> and follow me.
- 10:24 Children, how hard is it <u>for them that trust in riches</u> to enter into the kingdom of God.
- 11:26 <u>But if ye do not forgive, neither will your Father which is in heaven forgive your trespasses.</u>
- 13:14 But when ye shall see the abomination of desolation <u>spoken of by Daniel</u> the prophet.
- 13:33 Take ye heed, watch <u>and pray.</u>
- 14:68 And he went out into the porch; <u>and the cock crew.</u>
- 15:28 <u>And the scripture was fulfilled which saith, And he was numbered with</u> the transgressors.

Luke

- 1:28   the Lord is with thee: <u>blessed art thou among women.</u>
- 2:43   Jesus tarried behind in Jerusalem; and <u>Joseph and his mother</u> knew not of it.
- 4:8   And Jesus answered <u>and said unto him, Get thee behind me, Satan:</u>
- 9:54   Lord, wilt thou that we command fire to come down from heaven, and consume them, <u>even as Elias did?</u>
- 9:55   But he turned and rebuked them, <u>and said, Ye know not what manner of spirit ye are of.</u>
- 11:2-4 When ye pray, say, <u>Our</u> Father <u>which art in heaven,</u> Hallowed be thy name. Thy kingdom come. <u>Thy will be done, as in heaven,...so in earth but deliver us from evil.</u>
- 11:29 they seek a sign; and there shall no sign be given it but the sign of Jonas <u>the prophet.</u>
- 17:36 <u>Two men shall be in the field; the one shall be taken, and the other left.</u>
- 22:31 <u>And the Lord said,</u> Simon, Simon, behold, Satan hath <u>desired to have you.</u>
- 22:64 And when they had blindfolded him, <u>they struck him on the face.</u>
- 23:17 <u>For of necessity he must release one unto them at the feast.</u>
- 23:38 And a superscription also was written over him <u>in letters of Greek, and Latin, and Hebrew,</u> THIS IS THE KING OF THE JEWS.

John

- 1:27   He it is, who coming after me is preferred before me.
- 3:13   And no man hath ascended up to heaven, but he that came down from heaven, even the Son of man which is in heaven.
- 5:3-4   In these lay a great multitude of impotent folk, of blind, halt, withered, waiting for the moving of the water. For an angel went down at a certain season into the pool, and troubled the water: whosoever then first after the troubling of the water stepped in was made whole of whatsoever disease he had.
- 6:47   He that believeth on me hath everlasting life.
- 11:41   Then they took away the stone from the place where the dead was laid.
- 17:12   While I was with them in the world, I kept them in thy name.

Acts

- 10:6   he shall tell thee what thou oughtest to do.
- 20:32   And now, brethren, I commend you to God.
- 24:6-8   Who also hath gone about to profane the temple: whom we took, and would have judged according to our law. But the chief captain Lysias came upon us, and with great violence took him away out of our hands, Commanding his accusers to come unto thee.
- 24:15   there shall be a resurrection of the dead both of the just and unjust.
- 28:16   And when we came to Rome, the centurion delivered the prisoners to the captain of the guard.
- 28:29   And when he had said these words, the Jews departed and had great reasoning among themselves.

Romans

- 1:16   I am not ashamed of the Gospel of Christ.
- 9:28   For he will finish the work, and cut it short in righteousness: because a short work will the Lord make upon the earth.
- 10:15   How beautiful are the feet of them that preach the gospel of peace.
- 13:9   Thou shalt not steal, Thou shalt not bear false witness.
- 14:6   He that regardeth the day, regardeth it unto the Lord; and he that regardeth not the day, to the Lord he doth not regard it. He that eateth, eateth to the Lord, for he giveth God thanks.
- 14:21   whereby thy brother stumbleth, or is offended, or is made weak.
- 15:29   I shall come in the fullness of the blessing of the gospel of Christ.

I Corinthians

- 5:7   For even Christ our passover is sacrificed for us.
- 7:5   that ye may give yourselves to fasting and prayer.
- 7:39   The wife is bound by the law as long as her husband liveth.
- 11:24   Take, eat: this is my body, which is broken for you.

Galatians
- 3:1   who hath bewitched you, <u>that ye should not obey the truth</u>.

Ephesians
- 5:30 For we are members of his body, <u>of his flesh, and of his bones</u>.
- 6:10 Finally, <u>my brethren,</u> be strong in the Lord.

Philippians
- 3:16 Let us walk <u>by the same rule, let us mind the same thing.</u>

Colossians
- 1:14 In whom we have redemption <u>through his blood.</u>
- 3:6   the wrath of God cometh <u>on the children of disobedience.</u>

II Thessalonians
- 1:8   <u>In flaming fire</u> taking vengeance on them that know not God.

I Timothy
- 1:17 immortal, invisible, the only <u>wise</u> God.
- 4:12 in charity, <u>in spirit,</u> in faith, in purity.
- 6:5   destitute of the truth, supposing that gain is godliness: <u>from such withdraw thyself.</u>

II Timothy
- 1:11 I am appointed a preacher, and an apostle, and a teacher <u>of the Gentiles.</u>

Philemon
- 1:12 Whom I have sent again: <u>thou therefore receive him.</u>

Hebrews
- 1:3   when he had <u>by himself</u> purged our sins.
- 2:7   thou crownedst him with glory and honour <u>and didst set him over the works of thy hands.</u>
- 7:21   Thou art a priest for ever <u>after the order of Melchisedec.</u>
- 10:34 knowing in yourselves that ye have <u>in heaven</u> a better and an enduring substance.

I Peter
- 4:1   Christ hath suffered <u>for us</u> in the flesh.
- 4:14 <u>on their part he is evil spoken of, but on your part he is glorified.</u>
- 5:11 To him be <u>glory</u> and dominion for ever and ever. Amen.

II Peter
- 2:17 to whom the mist of darkness is reserved <u>for ever.</u>

I John
- 2:7   The old commandment is the word which ye have heard <u>from the beginning.</u>
- 5:7,8 For there are three that bear record <u>in heaven, the Father, the Word, and the Holy Ghost: and these three are one. 8 And there are three that bear</u>

witness in earth, the Spirit, and the water, and the blood: and these three agree in one.

Jude

- 25   To the only wise God our Saviour.

Revelation

- 2:13 I Know thy works, and where thou dwellest.
- 6:1   one of the four beasts saying Come and see. Also in verses 3, 5 and 7.
- 11:17 Saying, We give thee thanks O Lord God Almighty, which art, and wast, and art to come.
- 12:12 Woe to the inhabitants of the earth and of the sea.
- 16:17 there came a great voice out of the temple of heaven.
- 21:24 And the nations of them which are saved shall walk in the light of it: and the kings of the earth do bring their glory and honour into it.

None of the underlined words are in the text of the New International Version (1978 edition). Occasional reference is made to these omissions in the NIV footnotes. Many other words are omitted. And many others, which though included, are given a footnote expressing doubt. In fact as we will see the above list is only a very small part of the overall problem.

CHAPTER 2

Names of Christ Missing:
The Old Heresy

It is this fact of omitted Sacred Names that has often caused the first doubts over the modern Bibles. Names of Deity are missing and they are missing frequently! This in fact takes us back to an old heresy that began very in the history of the church.

Here are the total numbers of New Testament omissions in two of the most popular versions: The New American Standard and The New International. Where these Names are in combination, they have been counted separately.

	NASV	NIV
Jesus	73	36
Christ	43	44
Lord	35	35
God	33	31
Other Names	30	30
Total Missing Names	**214**	**176**

The KJV (mentioned first) is compared with the NIV:

Matthew 6:33
- But seek ye first the kingdom of God, and his righteousness.
- But seek first his kingdom and his righteousness.

Matthew 8:29
- And behold, they cried out saying, What have we to do with thee, Jesus, thou Son of God?
- What do you want with us, Son of God? they shouted.

Matthew 13:36
- Then Jesus sent the multitude away, and went into the house.
- Then he left the crowd and went into the house.

Matthew 13:51
• Jesus saith unto them, Have ye understood all these things? They say unto him, Yea, <u>Lord</u>.
• Have you understood all these things? Jesus asked. Yes, they replied.

Matthew 15:30
• And great multitudes came unto him, having with them those that were lame, blind, dumb, maimed, and many others, and cast them down at <u>Jesus'</u> feet; and he healed them.
• Great crowds came to him, bringing the lame, the blind, the crippled, the dumb and many others, and laid them at his feet; and he healed them.

Matthew 16:20
• Then charged he his disciples that they should tell no man that he was <u>Jesus</u> the Christ.
• Then he warned his disciples not to tell anyone that he was the Christ.

Matthew 17:20
• And <u>Jesus</u> said unto them, because of your unbelief,
•He replied, "Because you have so little faith.

Matthew 18:2
• And <u>Jesus</u> called a little child unto him.
•He called a little child.

Matthew 18:11
• <u>For the Son of man is come to save that which was lost.</u>
• Missing in the NIV.

Matthew 19:17
• And he said unto him, Why callest thou me good? there is none good but <u>one, that is God</u>.
• "Why do you ask me about what is good?" Jesus replied. "There is only One who is good."

Matthew 21:12
• And Jesus went into the temple <u>of God</u> and cast out all them that sold and bought.
• Jesus entered the temple area and drove out all who were buying and selling there.

Matthew 22:30
• For in the resurrection they neither marry, nor are given in marriage, but are as the angels <u>of God</u> in heaven.
• At the resurrection people will neither marry nor be given in marriage; they will be like the angels in heaven.

Matthew 22:32
• <u>God</u> is not the God of the dead, but of the living.

• He is not the God of the dead but of the living.

Matthew 23:8

• But be not ye called Rabbi: for one is your Master, <u>even Christ</u>.

•"But you are not to be called 'Rabbi', for you have only one Master".

Matthew 24:2

• And <u>Jesus</u> said unto them, See ye not all these things? Verily I say unto you, There shall not be left here one stone upon another.

• "Do you see all these things?" he asked. "I tell you the truth, not one stone here will be left on another.

Matthew 25:13

• Watch therefore, for ye know neither the day nor the hour <u>wherein the Son of man cometh</u>.

• Therefore keep watch, because you do not know the day or the hour.

Matthew 28:6

• He is not here: for he is risen, as he said. Come, see the place where <u>the Lord</u> lay.

• He is not here; he has risen, just as he said. Come and see the place where he lay.

The list continues by showing only the missing names:

Mark

• 5:13   And forthwith <u>Jesus</u> gave them leave.
• 6:33   And the people saw them departing, and many knew <u>him</u>, and ran afoot. thither out of all cities, and outwent them, and came together unto <u>him</u>.
• 7:27   But <u>Jesus</u> said unto her, Let the children first be filled.
• 9:24   The father of the child cried out, <u>and said with tears,</u> <u>Lord</u>.
• 11:10   Blessed be the kingdom of our father David, <u>that cometh in the name of the Lord</u>.
• 11:14   And <u>Jesus</u> answered and said unto it, No man eat fruit of thee.
• 11:26   <u>But if ye do not forgive, neither will your Father which is in heaven forgive your trespasses</u>.
• 12:27   He is not the God of the dead, but <u>the God</u> of the living.
• 14:45   and saith, Master, <u>master</u>; and kissed him.

Luke

• 2:40   And the child grew, and waxed strong <u>in spirit</u>.
• 4:4   man shall not live by bread alone, <u>but by every word of God</u>.

- 4:41   Thou art <u>Christ</u> the Son of God.
- 7:22   Then <u>Jesus</u> answering said unto them, Go your way.
- 7:31   <u>And the Lord said,</u> Whereunto then shall I liken the men of this generation?
- 9:56   <u>For the Son of man is not come to destroy men's lives, but to save them.</u>
- 9:57   <u>Lord,</u> I will follow thee whithersoever thou goest.
- 12:31   But rather seek ye the kingdom <u>of God.</u>
- 13:25   <u>Lord, Lord</u> open to us.
- 21:4   For all these have of their abundance cast in unto the offerings <u>of God.</u>
- 22:31   <u>And the Lord said,</u> Simon, Simon.
- 23:42   And he said unto <u>Jesus,</u> Lord, remember me.

John

- 4:16   <u>Jesus</u> saith unto her, Go, call thy husband.
- 4:42   and know that this is indeed <u>the Christ,</u> the Saviour of the world.
- 4:46   So <u>Jesus</u> came again into Cana of Galilee.
- 5:30   because I seek not mine own will, but the will of the <u>Father</u> which hath sent me.
- 6:39   And this is the <u>Father's</u> will which hath sent me.
- 6:69   And we believe and are sure that thou art that <u>Christ, the Son</u> of the living God.
- 8:20   These words spake <u>Jesus</u> in the treasury.
- 8:29   the <u>Father</u> hath not left me alone.
- 9:35   Dost thou believe on the <u>Son of God?</u>
- 16:16   a little while, and ye shall see me, <u>because I go to the Father.</u>
- 19:38   He came therefore, and took the body <u>of Jesus.</u>

Acts

- 2:30   <u>according to the flesh, he would raise up Christ</u> to sit on his throne.
- 3:26   Unto you first God, having raised up his <u>Son Jesus.</u>
- 4:24   Lord, <u>thou art God.</u>
- 7:30   there appeared to him in the wilderness of Mount Sina an angel <u>of the Lord.</u>
- 7:32   I am the God of thy fathers, the <u>God</u> of Abraham, and the God of Isaac, and the God of Jacob.
- 7:37   A prophet shall the <u>Lord</u> your God raise up unto you of your brethren like unto me; him shall ye hear.
- 8:37   <u>And Philip said, If thou believest with all thine heart, thou mayest. And he answered and said, I believe that Jesus Christ is the Son of God.</u>
- 9:5-6   And he said, Who art thou, Lord? And <u>the Lord</u> said, I am Jesus whom thou persecutest: <u>It is hard for thee to kick against the pricks. And he</u>

trembling and astonished said, Lord, what wilt thou have me to do? And the Lord said unto him, Arise.

- 9:29 And he spake boldly in the name of the Lord Jesus.
- 15:11 through the grace of the Lord Jesus Christ we shall be saved, even as they.
- 15:18 Known unto God are all his works from the beginning of the world.
- 16:31 Believe on the Lord Jesus Christ and thou shalt be saved.
- 19:4 that they should believe on him which should come after him, that is, on Christ Jesus.
- 19:10 so that all they which dwelt in Asia heard the word of the Lord Jesus.
- 20:21 repentance toward God, and faith toward our Lord Jesus Christ.
- 20:25 among whom I have gone preaching the kingdom of God.
- 22:16 wash away thy sins, calling on the name of the Lord.
- 23:9 let us not fight against God.

Romans

- 1:16 For I am not ashamed of the gospel of Christ.
- 6:11 alive unto God through Jesus Christ our Lord.
- 8:1 There is therefore now no condemnation to them which are in Christ. Jesus, who walk not after the flesh, but after the Spirit.
- 14:6 He that regardeth the day, regardeth it unto the Lord; and he that regardeth not the day, to the Lord he doth not regard it. He that eateth, eateth to the Lord.
- 15:8 Now I say that Jesus Christ was a minister of the circumcision.
- 15:19 Through mighty signs and wonders, by the power of the Spirit of God.
- 16:18 For they that are such serve not our Lord Jesus Christ.
- 16:24 The grace of our Lord Jesus Christ be with you all. Amen.

I Corinthians

- 1:14 I thank God that I baptized none of you.
- 5:4 In the name of our Lord Jesus Christ, when ye are gathered together.
- 5:5 that the spirit may be saved in the day of the Lord Jesus.
- 6:20 glorify God in your body and in your spirit, which are God's.
- 9:1 have I not seen Jesus Christ our Lord?
- 9:18 Verily that, when I preach the gospel, I may make the gospel of Christ without charge.
- 10:28 for the earth is the Lord's and the fullness thereof.
- 15:47 the second man is the Lord from heaven.
- 16:22 If any man love not the Lord Jesus Christ, let him be Anathema.
- 16:23 The grace of our Lord Jesus Christ be with you.

II Corinthians
- 4:6   the glory of God in the face of <u>Jesus</u> Christ.
- 4:10   Always bearing about in the body the dying of <u>the Lord</u> Jesus.
- 5:18   hath reconciled us to himself by <u>Jesus</u> Christ.
- 10:7   that, as he is <u>Christ's</u>, even so are we Christ's.
- 11:31   The God and Father of <u>our</u> Lord Jesus <u>Christ</u>.

Galatians
- 3:17   the covenant, that was confirmed before of God <u>in Christ</u>.
- 4:7   heir of God <u>through Christ</u>.
- 6:15   For <u>in Christ Jesus</u> neither circumcision availeth any thing.
- 6:17   I bear in my body the marks of <u>the Lord Jesus.</u>

Ephesians
- 3:9   God, who created all things <u>by Jesus Christ</u>.
- 3:14   I bow my knees unto the Father <u>of our Lord Jesus Christ</u>.
- 5:9   For the fruit of <u>the Spirit</u> is in all goodness.

Philippians
- 4:13   I can do all things through <u>Christ</u>.

Colossians
- 1:2   peace, from God our Father <u>and the Lord Jesus Christ</u>.
- 1:28   that we may present every man perfect in Christ <u>Jesus.</u>
- 2:2   to the acknowledgment of the mystery of God, and of the <u>Father</u>, and of Christ.

I Thessalonians
- 1:1   peace, from <u>God our Father, and the Lord Jesus Christ.</u>
- 2:19   in the presence of our Lord Jesus <u>Christ</u> at his coming?
- 3:11   Now God himself and our Father, and our Lord Jesus <u>Christ.</u>
- 3:13   at the coming of our Lord Jesus <u>Christ</u> with all his saints.

II Thessalonians
- 1:8   that obey not the gospel of our Lord Jesus <u>Christ</u>.
- 1:12   That the name of our Lord Jesus <u>Christ</u> may be glorified.
- 2:4   so that he <u>as God</u> sitteth in the temple of God.

I Timothy
- 1:1   and <u>Lord</u> Jesus Christ, which is our hope.
- 2:7   speak the truth <u>in Christ</u>, and lie not.
- 3:16   And without controversy great is the mystery of godliness: <u>God</u> was manifest in the flesh.
- 5:21   I charge thee before God, and the <u>Lord</u> Jesus Christ.

II Timothy
- 4:1   I charge thee therefore before God and <u>the Lord</u> Jesus Christ.
- 4:22   The Lord <u>Jesus Christ</u> be with thy spirit.

Titus
- 1:4   from God the Father and the <u>Lord</u> Jesus Christ our Saviour.

Philemon
- 6   every good thing which is in you in Christ <u>Jesus</u>.

Hebrews
- 3:1   the Apostle and High Priest of our profession, <u>Christ</u> Jesus.
- 10:9   Then said he, Lo, I come to do thy will, <u>O God</u>.
- 10:30 I will recompense, <u>saith the Lord</u>.

I Peter
- 1:22   Seeing ye have purified your souls in obeying the truth <u>through the Spirit</u>.
- 5:10   who hath called us unto his eternal glory by Christ <u>Jesus.</u>
- 5:14   Peace be with you all that are in Christ <u>Jesus. Amen.</u>

I John
- 1:7   the blood of Jesus <u>Christ</u> his Son cleanseth us from all sin.
- 3:16   Hereby perceive we the love <u>of God</u>.
- 4:3   And every spirit that confesseth not that Jesus <u>Christ is come in the flesh</u> is not of God.
- 5:7-8 For there are three that bear record in heaven, <u>the Father, the Word, and the Holy Ghost: and these three are one. And there are three that bear witness in earth</u>, the Spirit, and the water, and the blood: and these   three agree in one.
- 5:13   <u>and that ye may believe on the name of the Son of God.</u>

II John
- 3   and from the <u>Lord</u> Jesus Christ.
- 9   He that abideth in the doctrine <u>of Christ</u>, he hath both the Father and the Son.

Jude
- 4   denying the only <u>Lord</u> God, and our Lord Jesus Christ.

Revelation
- 1:8   I am Alpha and Omega, <u>the beginning and the ending.</u>
- 1:9   the kingdom and patience of Jesus <u>Christ</u> and for the testimony of Jesus Christ.
- 1:11   Saying, <u>I am Alpha and Omega, the first and the last.</u>
- 5:14   <u>the four and twenty elders fell down and worshipped him that liveth for ever and ever.</u>
- 12:17 and have the testimony of Jesus <u>Christ.</u>
- 14:5   they are without fault <u>before the throne of God.</u>
- 16:5   Thou art righteous, <u>O Lord,</u> which art, and wast, and shalt be.
- 19:1   glory, and honour, and power, unto <u>the Lord</u> our God.

- 20:9   and there came down from <u>God out</u> of heaven, and devoured them.
- 20:12 And I saw the dead, small and great, stand before <u>God.</u>
- 21:4   And <u>God</u> shall wipe away all tears from their eyes.
- 22:21 The grace of our Lord Jesus <u>Christ</u> be with you all. Amen.

Defenders of the modern versions have sought to minimize the fact of these missing Names of Deity. Dr. Homer Kent, former president of Grace Theological Seminary in Indiana is typical. He says in his tract *The King James Only?*

> One common objection is that in a relatively few cases
> the names "Christ" and "Lord" are omitted when referring
> to Jesus.

Whatever arguments one might attempt to raise, the above evidence demonstrates that these Names are missing more than in a "relatively few cases"! In fact, what has been shown above is only part of the story and introduces us now to the primary error in the Modern Version controversy.

CHAPTER 3

ADOPTIONISM:
The Old Heresy Behind the Text
of the Modern Versions

By going through the above verses two important trends appear.

1.   The Name "Jesus" is frequently disassociated from the titles "Lord" and "Christ." Whereas in the AV we will read "Jesus Christ" or the "Lord Jesus Christ," in the Modern Versions "Jesus" is often made to stand alone or not at all. In fact, our Saviour's full title "Lord Jesus Christ" is found 84 times in 81 verses in the AV and only 60 times in 60 verses in the NIV, 62 times in 62 verses in the NRSV, and 63 times in 63 verses in the RSV. A noticeable difference is clearly apparent!

2.   In the above list the name "Jesus" is frequently removed from statements of Deity and works of Deity.

Looking at Matthew and Mark,
Jesus is removed from:

Matthew
- 4:12   The prophesy of the great light (12-16).
- 4:18   The call to discipleship (18-22).
- 4:23   The miracle working ministry in Galilee (23-25).
- 8:29   Association with the title "thou Son of God."
- 12:25 The healing of the blind and dumb demoniac (22-30).
- 13:36 The interpretation of wheat and tares (36-43).
- 13:51 Association with the title "Lord" (which is also removed).
- 14:14 The immediate account of a miracle.
- 14:22 Much of the account of walking on the sea (22-27).
- 15:16 The discourse about defilement (10-20).
- 15:30 The immediate account of a miracle.
- 16:20 Association with the title "the Christ.".

Mark

- 1:41   The immediate account of a miracle.
- 5:13   The immediate account of a miracle.
- 5:19   Association with the title "Lord."
- 6:34   The feeding of the 5,000 (32-44).
- 7:27   The healing of the Syrophenician woman's daughter (24-30).
- 8:1   The feeding of the 4,000 (1-9).
- 8:17   The discourse concerning leaven (14-21).
- 11:14 The cursing of the fig tree (12-14).
- 11:15 The cleansing of the Temple (15-19).
- 12:41 The account of the widow's mite (41-44).
- 14:22 The account of the Last Supper (22-25).

In the author's, *Early Manuscripts, Church Fathers, and the Authorized Version* (Available from the Bible For Today) eighty-six examples of this disassociation are given.

What Lies Behind This Separation?

This separation of "Jesus" from "Christ" occurs far too often to look for a cause other than deliberate editing in certain N.T. manuscripts. That there was a strong movement in the early centuries that could result in such a systematic editing; there can be no doubt! The foremost error regarding the Person of Christ is to deny His true Deity and true Humanity. The chief means by which this was done, and which finds expression down to our own day, is technically known as "Adoptionism" or "Spirit Christology." The heresy follows this line of reasoning: Jesus of Nazareth, an ordinary man of unusual virtue, was "adopted" by God into divine Sonship by the advent of the "Christ-Spirit" at His baptism. Therefore, <u>Jesus became Christ</u> at His baptism rather than the fact that He was always the Christ from eternity. And, though united for a time, Jesus and Christ were separate personages. Many names and groups are associated with this wicked teaching, foremost of whom were the Gnostics. The liberal J. N. D. Kelly writes,

> There was a great variety of Gnostic systems, but a common pattern ran through them all. From the pleroma, or spiritual world of aeons, the divine Christ descended and united Himself for a time (according to Ptolemy, between the baptism and the passion) to the historical personage. These were tendencies on the fringe, yet Gnosticism at any rate came within an ace of swamping the central tradition. (Early

Christian Doctrines, London: Adam & Charles Black, 1958, pp. 141,142).

Ponder carefully Kelly's statement about how near this came to "swamping the central tradition"! In the summaries, we will be looking more closely at Egypt; but notice for now that Kelly's mention of Ptolemy and Gnosticism takes us to that city that gave powerful force and rise to the Gnostic error - Alexandria.

It is for this reason that the Bible closes with the following warnings:

- 1 John. 2:22   Who is a liar but he that denieth that Jesus is the Christ?
- 1 John. 4:2, 3   Every spirit that confesseth that Jesus Christ is come in the flesh is of God: And every spirit that confesseth not that Jesus Christ is come in the flesh is not of God; and this is that spirit of antichrist.
- 1 John. 5:1   Whosoever believeth that Jesus is the Christ is born of God.
- 2 John. 7   For many deceivers are entered into the world, who confess not that Jesus Christ is come in the flesh: This is a deceiver and an antichrist.

The terrible heresy has found expression in a number of ways down through the centuries, and it has been given a new lease on life through the Modern Versions. This then is the *old heresy revived*!

Psalms 117:1-2 O praise the LORD, all ye nations: praise him, all ye people. For his merciful kindness is great toward us: and the truth of the LORD endureth for ever. Praise ye the LORD.

CHAPTER 4

Further Significant Passages Missing

Very few Christians are aware as to how much is actually missing in the modern Bibles and what the consequence actually is. With this next list the extent of the problem can now begin to be realized. Yet even after showing the following, there is a great deal more yet to come. The underlined portions are omitted in the New International Version and most other Twentieth Century versions both in English and other languages.

Matthew

- 5:22 whosoever is angry with his brother <u>without a cause</u> shall be in danger.
- 5:27 Ye have heard that it was said <u>by them of old time</u>, Thou shalt not commit adultery.
- 6:4 thy Father which seeth in secret himself shall reward thee <u>openly</u>.
- 6:6 thy Father which seeth in secret shall reward thee <u>openly</u>.
- 6:18 and thy father, which seeth in secret, shall reward thee <u>openly</u>.
- 15:6 And honour not his father <u>or his mother</u>.
- 19:16 <u>Good</u> Master, what good thing shall I do.
- 19:20 All these things have I kept <u>from my youth up</u>.
- 20:23 Ye shall drink indeed of my cup, <u>and be baptized with the baptism that I am baptized with</u>.
- 20:34 and immediately <u>their eyes</u> received sight, and they followed him.
- 22:7 But when the king <u>heard</u> thereof, he was wroth.
- 22:13 Bind him hand and foot, <u>and take him away</u>, and cast him into outer darkness.
- 23:4 For they bind heavy burdens <u>and grievous to be borne</u>.
- 23:19, Ye <u>fools and</u> blind; for whether is greater.
- 24:7 and there shall be famines, <u>and pestilences</u>, and earthquakes, in divers places.
- 24:48 that evil servant shall say in his heart, My lord delayeth <u>his coming</u>.
- 25:31 When the Son of man shall come in his glory, and all the <u>holy</u> angels with him.

- 26:3   Then assembled together the chief priests, and the scribes, and the elders.
- 26:28 For this is my blood of the new testament, which is shed.
- 26:59 Now the chief priests, and elders, and all the council.
- 26:60 But found none; yea, though many false witnesses came, yet found they none.
- 27:42 If he be the King of Israel, let him now come down from the cross.
- 27:64 lest his disciples come by night, and steal him away.

Mark

- 1:42   And as soon as he had spoken, immediately the leprosy departed.
- 2:16   they said unto his disciples, How is it that he eateth and drinketh?
- 2:22   else the new wine doth burst the bottles, and the wine is spilled.
- 3:15   And to have power to heal sicknesses and to cast out devils.
- 4:11   unto you it is given to know the mystery of the kingdom of God.
- 6:36   and buy themselves bread: for they have nothing to eat.
- 7:2   that is to say, with unwashen hands, they found fault.
- 8:9   And they that had eaten were about four thousand.
- 8:26   Neither go into the town, nor tell it to any in the town.
- 9:29   This kind can come forth by nothing, but by prayer and fasting.
- 9:45   then having two feet to be cast into hell, into the fire that never shall be quenched.
- 9:49   For every one shall be salted with fire, and every sacrifice shall be salted with salt.
- 10:21 and come, take up the cross, and follow me.
- 11:8   and others cut down branches off the trees, and strawed them in the way.
- 11:23 those things which he saith shall come to pass; he shall have whatsoever he saith.
- 12:4   at him they cast stones, and wounded him in the head, and sent him away shamefully handled.
- 12:23 In the resurrection therefore, when they shall rise, whose wife shall she be of them?
- 12:29 The first of all the commandments is, Hear, O Israel.
- 12:30 and with all thy strength: this is the first commandment.
- 12:33 and with all the understanding, and with all the soul.
- 13:8   and there shall be famines and troubles.
- 13:11 take no thought beforehand what ye shall speak, neither do ye premeditate.
- 14:19 to say unto him one by one, Is it I? and another said, Is it I?
- 14:22 Take, eat: this is my body.
- 14:24 This is my blood of the new testament, which is shed for many.

- 14:27 All ye shall be offended <u>because of me this night</u>.
- 14:51 <u>and the young men</u> laid hold on him.
- 14:70 thou art a Galilaean, <u>and thy speech agreeth thereto</u>.
- 15:3 accused him of many things: <u>but he answered nothing</u>.
- 15:39 saw that <u>he so cried out</u>, and gave up the ghost.

Luke

- 1:29 And <u>when she saw him</u>, she was troubled at his saying.
- 2:42 they went <u>up to Jerusalem</u> after the custom of the feast.
- 4:18 he hath sent me <u>to heal the brokenhearted</u>, to preach deliverance.
- 5:38 But new wine must be put into new bottles; <u>and both are preserved</u>.
- 7:28 there is not a greater <u>prophet</u> than John the Baptist.
- 8:43 And a woman having an issue of blood twelve years, which <u>had spent all her living upon physicians</u>.
- 8:45 When all denied, Peter <u>and they that were with him</u> said, Master, the multitude throng thee and press thee, <u>and sayest thou, Who touched</u> me?
- 8:48 <u>be of good comfort</u>: thy faith hath made thee whole; go in peace.
- 8:54 And <u>he put them all out</u>, and took her by the hand.
- 9:10 And he took them, and went aside privately into <u>a desert place</u> belonging to the city called Bethsaida.
- 11:11 If a son shall ask <u>bread of any of you</u> that is a father, will he give him a stone? or if he ask a fish.
- 11:44 Woe unto you, <u>scribes and Pharisees, hypocrites</u>!
- 11:54 seeking to catch something out of his mouth, <u>that they might accuse him</u>.
- 12:39 had known what hour the thief would come, <u>he would have watched</u>, and not have suffered his house to be broken through.
- 17:3 If thy brother trespass <u>against thee</u>, rebuke him.
- 17:9 that were commanded <u>him? I trow not</u>.
- 18:24 And when Jesus saw <u>that he was very sorrowful</u>, he said.
- 19:45 and began to cast out them that sold <u>therein, and them that bought</u>.
- 20:13 it may be they will reverence him <u>when they see him</u>.
- 20:23 But he perceived their craftiness, and said unto them, <u>Why tempt ye me</u>?
- 20:30 And the second <u>took her to wife, and he died childless</u>.
- 22:68 ye will not answer <u>me, nor let me go</u>.
- 23:23 And the voices of them <u>and of the chief priests</u> prevailed.
- 24:1 spices which they had prepared, <u>and certain others with them</u>.
- 24:46 Thus it is written <u>and thus it behoved</u> Christ to suffer.

John

- 1:51 <u>Hereafter</u> ye shall see heaven open.
- 3:15 <u>should not perish</u>, but have eternal life.

- 5:16   therefore did the Jews persecute Jesus, <u>and sought to slay him.</u>
- 6:11   he distributed <u>to the disciples, and the disciples</u> to them.
- 6:22   save <u>that one whereinto his disciples</u> were entered.
- 6:65   except it were given unto him of <u>my</u> Father.
- 8:9   <u>being convicted by their own conscience,</u> went out one by one, beginning at the eldest, even unto the last.
- 8:10   When Jesus had lifted up himself, <u>and saw none but the woman,</u> he said unto her, Woman, where are <u>those thine accusers?</u>
- 8:28   but as <u>my</u> Father hath taught me, I speak these things.
- 8:38   I speak that which I have seen with <u>my</u> Father.
- 8:59   and went out of the temple, <u>going through the midst of them, and so passed by.</u>
- 9:6   and he anointed the eyes of the <u>blind</u> man with the clay.
- 10:26 because ye are not of my sheep, <u>as I said unto you.</u>
- 12:1   where Lazarus was <u>which had been dead.</u>
- 14:28 I go unto the Father: for <u>my</u> Father is greater than I.
- 16:10 because I go to <u>my</u> Father.
- 17:17 Sanctify them through thy truth: <u>thy</u> word is truth.
- 18:40 Then cried they <u>all</u> again, saying.
- 19:16 And they took Jesus, <u>and led him away.</u>
- 20:17 for I am not yet ascended to <u>my</u> Father.

Acts

- 3:11   And as <u>the lame man which was healed</u> held Peter and John.
- 5:16   There came also a multitude out of the cities round about <u>unto</u> Jerusalem.
- 6:13   This man ceaseth not to speak <u>blasphemous</u> words against this holy place, and the law.
- 7:37   A prophet shall the Lord your God raise up unto you of your brethren, like unto me: <u>him shall ye hear.</u>
- 10:12 Wherein were all manner of fourfooted beasts of the earth, and <u>wild beasts.</u>
- 10:21 Then Peter went down to the men <u>which were sent unto him from Cornelius.</u>
- 10:30 Four days ago I was <u>fasting</u> until this hour.
- 10:32 he is lodged in the house of one Simon a tanner by the sea side: <u>who, when he cometh, shall speak unto thee.</u>
- 13:45 spake against those things which were spoken by Paul, <u>contradicting and blaspheming.</u>
- 15:23 And they wrote letters by them <u>after this manner.</u>
- 15:24 subverting your souls, saying, <u>Ye must be circumcised, and keep the law.</u>

- 17:5   But the Jews <u>which believed not</u>, moved with envy, took unto them.
- 17:26 And hath made of one <u>blood</u> all nations of men.
- 18:17 Then all <u>the Greeks</u> took Sosthenes.
- 18:21 But bade them farewell, saying, <u>I must by all means keep this feast that cometh in Jerusalem.</u>
- 20:15 we arrived at Samos, and <u>tarried at Trogyllium.</u>
- 21:8   And the next day we <u>that were of Paul's company</u> departed.
- 21:22 What is it therefore? <u>the multitude must needs come together</u>: for they will hear.
- 21:25 we have written and concluded <u>that they observe no such thing</u>, save only that they keep themselves from.
- 22:9   And they that were with me saw indeed the light, <u>and were afraid.</u>
- 22:20 I also was standing by, and consenting <u>unto his death.</u>
- 22:26 and told the chief captain, saying, <u>Take heed</u> what thou doest.
- 23:12 And when it was day, <u>certain</u> of the Jews banded together.
- 23:15 that he bring him down unto you <u>to morrow</u>.
- 24:26 He hoped also that money should have been given him of Paul, <u>that he might loose him.</u>
- 25:16 to deliver any man <u>to die</u>, before that he which is accused.
- 26:30 <u>And when he had thus spoken</u>, the king rose up.
- 28:16 And when we came to Rome, <u>the centurion delivered the prisoners to the captain of the guard.</u>

Romans
- 9:32   they sought it not by faith, but as it were by the works <u>of the law.</u>
- 11:6   no more of works: otherwise grace is no more grace. <u>But if it be of works, then is it no more grace: otherwise work is no more work.</u>
- 15:24 Whensoever I take my journey into Spain, <u>I will come to you</u>.
- 15:29 I shall come in the fullness of the blessing <u>of the gospel</u> of Christ.

I Corinthians
- 6:20   glorify God in your body, <u>and in your spirit, which are God's.</u>
- 7:39   The wife is bound <u>by the law</u> as long as her husband liveth.
- 9:22   To the weak became I <u>as</u> weak.
- 10:28 conscience sake: <u>for the earth is the Lord's, and the fullness thereof.</u>

II Corinthians
- 5:17   old things are passed away; behold, <u>all things</u> are become new.

Galatians
- 5:19   <u>Adultery,</u> fornication, uncleanness, lasciviousness.
- 5:21   Envyings, <u>murders,</u> drunkenness.

Ephesians
- 4:9   that he also descended <u>first</u> into the lower parts of the earth?

- 4:17   that ye henceforth walk not as <u>other</u> Gentiles walk.

Colossians

- 2:18   intruding into those things which he hath <u>not</u> seen.

I Thessalonians

- 2:15   Who both killed the Lord Jesus, and <u>their own prophets</u>.

I Timothy

- 5:4   for that is <u>good and acceptable</u> before God.
- 5:16   If any <u>man or</u> woman that believeth have widows.
- 6:7   into this world, <u>and it is certain</u> we can carry nothing out.

Titus

- 1:4   Grace, <u>mercy</u>, and peace, from God the Father.

Hebrews

- 2:7   thou crownedst him with glory and honour, <u>and didst set him over the works of thy hands</u>.
- 3:6   if we hold fast the confidence and the rejoicing of the hope <u>firm unto the end</u>.
- 8:12   and their sins <u>and their iniquities</u> will I remember no more.
- 10:34 that ye have <u>in heaven</u> a better and an enduring substance.
- 11:11 received strength to conceive seed, and was <u>delivered of a child</u> when she was past age.
- 11:13 but having seen them afar off, <u>and were persuaded of them</u>.
- 12:20 touch the mountain, it shall be stoned <u>or thrust through with a dart</u>.
- 13:21 Make you perfect in every good <u>work</u> to do his will.

James

- 4:4   Ye <u>adulterers and</u> adulteresses, know ye not.
- 5:5   ye have nourished your hearts, <u>as</u> in a day of slaughter.

I Peter

- 3:16   whereas they speak evil of you, <u>as of evildoers</u>.
- 4:3   For the time past <u>of our life</u> may suffice us.
- 5:5   Yea, all of you <u>be subject</u> one to another.

II Peter

- 3:10   But the day of the Lord will come as a thief <u>in the night</u>.

Revelation

- 2:3   for my name's sake <u>hast laboured</u>, and hast not fainted.
- 2:9   I know thy <u>works, and tribulation</u>.
- 2:13   I know <u>thy works, and</u> where thou dwellest.
- 2:20   Notwithstanding I have a <u>few things</u> against thee.
- 5:4   no man was found worthy to open <u>and to read</u> the book.
- 11:1   <u>and the angel stood</u>, saying, Rise, and measure the temple of God.
- 13:10 He that <u>leadeth</u> into captivity shall go into captivity.

- 15:2   and them that had gotten the victory over the beast, and over his image, and <u>over his mark</u>.
- 16:17 and there came a great voice out of the temple of <u>heaven</u>.
- 19:1   Alleluia; Salvation, and glory, <u>and honour</u>, and power, unto the Lord.

Psalms 12:6-7 The words of the LORD are pure words: as silver tried in a furnace of earth, purified seven times. Thou shalt keep them, O LORD, thou shalt preserve them from this generation for ever.

CHAPTER 5

Hell Missing

The doctrine of eternal hell is a fearful Bible truth. The word itself has from the beginning of the English language had a fixed and established meaning. *"The wicked shall be turned into hell and all the nations that forget God"* (Psalm 9:17) is plain. In fact, for many (including preachers and Bible translators) it appears to be too plain. Many today do not mind using the word in their daily conversation, but do not like seeing it in the Bible.

Modern translations seem to have tried to make the Bible more acceptable by taking some of the terror out of the fact that a man or woman who dies outside of faith in Jesus Christ will go to an eternal and conscious hell. Translators have done this in two ways. First, the word is often left in its untranslated Hebrew or Greek form (Sheol, Hades), and thus its impact upon an English reader is diminished. The New American Standard Bible reverts to this practice. Secondly, some simply translate Sheol as "death" or "grave." The Jehovah's Witness "Bible" does this, and (if you can believe it!) so does the New International Version.

In the previous lists, the point at issue has been the underlying Greek text of the New Testament. The modern versions are based on a different text than the KJV. This as we will explain in the following chapters is the reason for the many omissions. Here, though, the issue is generally not the underlying text, but rather the philosophy of the translators. In the case of the NIV translators, their philosophical choice has been to completely take hell out of the Old Testament!

"Hell" in the KJV (mentioned first) and NIV

Deuteronomy 32:22
- For a fire is kindled in mine anger, and shall burn into the lowest <u>hell</u>.
- For a fire has been kindled by my wrath, one that burns to the realm of <u>death</u> below.

2 Samuel 22:6
- The sorrows of <u>hell</u> compassed me about.
- The cords of the <u>grave</u> coiled around me.

Job 11:8
- It is as high as heaven; what canst thou do? deeper than <u>hell</u>; what canst thou know?
- They are higher than the heavens-what can you do? They are deeper than the depths of the <u>grave</u>-what can you know?

Job 26:6
- <u>Hell</u> is naked before him.
- <u>Death</u> naked before God.

Psalm 9:17
- The wicked shall be turned into <u>Hell</u>, and all the nations that forget God.
- The wicked return to the <u>grave</u>, all nations that forget God.

Psalm 16:10
- For thou wilt not leave my soul in <u>hell</u>; neither wilt thou suffer thine Holy One to see corruption.
- Because you will not abandon me to the <u>grave</u>, nor will you let your Holy One see decay.

Psalm 18:5
- The sorrows of <u>hell</u> compassed me about: the snares of death prevented me.
- The cords of the <u>grave</u> coiled around me; the snares of death confronted me.

Psalm 55:15
- Let death seize upon them, and let them go down quick into <u>hell</u>.
- Let death take my enemies by surprise; let them go down alive to the <u>grave</u>.

Psalm 86:13
- thou hast delivered my soul from the lowest <u>hell</u>.
- you have delivered my soul from the depths of the <u>grave</u>.

Psalm 116:3
- The sorrows of death compassed me, and the pains of <u>hell</u> gat hold upon me.
- The cords of death entangled me, the anguish of the <u>grave</u> came upon me.

Psalm 139:8
- If I ascend up into heaven, thou art there: if I make my bed in <u>hell</u>, behold, thou art there.
- If I go up to the heavens, you are there; if I make my bed in the <u>depths</u>, you are there.

Proverbs 5:5
- Her feet go down to death; her steps take hold on <u>hell</u>.
- Her feet go down to death; her steps lead straight to the <u>grave</u>.

Proverbs 7:27
- Her house is the way to hell, going down to the chambers of <u>death</u>.

- Her house is a highway to the grave, dealing down to the chambers of death.

Proverbs 9:18
- her guests are in the depths of hell.
- her guests are in the depths of the grave.

Proverbs 15:11
- Hell and destruction are before the Lord.
- Death and Destruction lie open before the Lord.

Proverbs 15:24
- The way of life is above to the wise, that he may depart from hell beneath.
- The path of life leads upward for the wise to keep him from going down to the grave.

Proverbs 23:14
- and shalt deliver his soul from hell.
- and save his soul from death.

Proverbs 27:20
- Hell and destruction are never full.
- Death and Destruction are never satisfied.

Isaiah 5:14
- Therefore hell hath enlarged herself, and opened her mouth without measure.
- Therefore the grave enlarges its appetite and opens its mouth without limit.

Isaiah 14:9
- Hell from beneath is moved for thee to meet thee at thy coming: it stirreth up the dead for thee, even all the chief ones of the earth.
- The grave below is all astir to meet you at your coming; it rouses the spirits of the departed to greet you-all those who were leaders in the world.

Isaiah 14:15
- Yet thou shalt be brought down to hell, to the sides of the pit.
- But you are brought down to the grave, to the depths of the pit.

Isaiah 28:15
- Because ye have said, We have made a covenant with death, and with hell are we at agreement.
- You boast, "We have entered into a covenant with death, with the grave we have made an agreement."

Isaiah 28:18
- And your covenant with death shall be disannulled and your agreement with hell shall not stand.
- Your covenant with death will be annulled; your agreement with the grave will not stand.

Isaiah 57:9

- and didst debase thyself even unto hell.
- you descended to the grave itself.

Ezekiel 31:16

- I cast him down to hell with them that descend into the pit.
- I brought it down to the grave with those who go down to the pit.

Ezekiel 31:17

- They also went down into hell.
- had also gone down to the grave.

Ezekiel 32:21

- The strong among the mighty shall speak to him out of the midst of hell.
- From within the grave the mighty leaders will say.

Ezekiel 32:27

- which are gone down to hell.
- who went down to the grave.

Amos 9:2

- Though they dig into hell, thence shall mine hand take them.
- Though they dig down to the depths of the grave, from there my hand take them.

Jonah 2:2

- out of the belly of hell cried I, and thou heardest my voice.
- From the depths of the grave I called for help.

Habakkuk 2:5

- who enlargeth his desire as hell, and is as death.
- because he is as greedy as the grave and like death.

In the New Testament the word hell is found twenty-two times in the Authorised Version, compared with thirteen in the New International Version. But the biggest shock comes when we see how this popular translation completely removes hell from the Old Testament. Yes, the Modern Bibles have gotten rid of the "Thee's" and "Thou's" and a lot else!

CHAPTER 6

How Many Missing Words?

A most striking fact about the Modern Bibles is that in the New Testament they are clearly shorter than the Authorised Version. The following, by comparing the Greek texts which underlie the AV and Modern Versions, gives an idea of how much shorter. The primary basis of the Modern Version Text is The Nestle Aland Greek New Testament. Its text is identical to another popular edition published by The United Bible Society. The KJV New Testament is based on what is known as the Received Text. A widely published edition of the Received Text was that prepared by Robert Stephanus in 1550. The KJV does not follow Stephanus in every instance, nor is the NIV completely identical with the Nestle Aland, but these two editions provide a good basis for comparison. In an actual chapter-by-chapter count made by Mrs. Catherine Carmichael in our Bible Institute in Johannesburg back in 1985 the following figures were derived.

Stephanus Received Text (listed first) compared with Nestle-Aland

Matthew	18,740	18,359	-381 fewer words
Mark	11,646	11,268	-78
Luke	19,935	19,473	-462
John	15,957	15,636	-321
Acts	18,794	18,448	-346
Romans	7,204	7,108	-96
I Corinthians	6,933	6,830	-103
II Corinthians	4,509	4,476	-33
Galatians	2,251	2,231	-20
Ephesians	2,462	2,421	-41
Philippians	1,641	1,629	-12
Colossians	1,621	1,581	-40
I Thess.	1,495	1,481	-14
II Thess.	834	819	-15
I Timothy	1,624	1,591	-33
II Timothy	1,254	1,238	-16

Titus	666	659	-7
Philemon	339	334	-5
Hebrews	4,990	4,953	-37
James	1,763	1,742	-21
I Peter	1,724	1,684	-40
II Peter	1,104	1,099	-5
I John	2,175	2,141	-34
II John	249	245	-4
III John	218	219	+1
Jude	452	461	+9
Revelation	9,941	9,851	-90
Subtotal	**140,521**	**137,977***	**-2,544***

*The modern versions either omit, place in the footnotes, question their authenticity, or place in brackets, Mark 16:9-20 and John 7:53-8:11. After taking these two well-known passages into account the final count is:

Final Total   140,521   137,602   -2,886 fewer words

In the New Testament the modern version text is shorter than that of the King James Version by about the number of words contained in I and II Peter!

CHAPTER 7

How Many Different Kinds Of Variations?

Omissions are only part of the story! In fact when comparing the Greek Text of the KJV with that of the modern versions, omissions account for only about ONE THIRD of the total variations between the two!

Today the commonly used edition of the Received Text is that which was edited at the end of the 19th Century by H. A. Scrivener: *The Greek Text Underlying the English Authorised Version of 1611*. In our book *8000 Differences* (available from the Bible For Today) a line upon line comparison is made between this edition and the Nestle-Aland Text. A total of 8,032 *variation units* are listed.

A variation unit may involve:
- the spelling of a word
- substitution by different words
- interchange of the same words in a sentence
- frequently, the removal of words
- at times, the addition of words

Therefore, a variation unit may comprise anything from one word, to a clause, to a verse, to (as in the case of Mark 16) a number of verses. These 8000+ differences do not include the many occurrences of a stylistic scribal addition at the end of a word known as the *moveable nu*.

If it be argued that some of the differences are insignificant, and may for example "only" be a variation in the spelling of a word, we answer that it will affect the sound and frequently the inflection and structure of the Greek sentence. When we believe that "*all* Scripture is given by inspiration of God" (II Tim. 3:16), and that "*every* word of God is pure" (Prov. 30:5), questions will not be raised as to which differences are significant or insignificant. If this is how God breathed out His Words, then it is significant! Further, as we will show, a denial of the Scripture's teaching concerning its own verbal preservation will weaken belief in verbal inspiration.

The variation will often affect the English translation. Where the variation is not translatable, a search of the list will show that the underlying text is frequently weakened or lessened in some way. This is much like having green grass, but with the root structure beneath compromised.

"The Single Sheet of Paper"

Speaking of the revised Greek text, its chief architect F. J. A. Hort sought to dampen down the extent of the changes by claiming that "the amount of what can in any sense be called substantial variation is but a small fraction of the whole residuary variation, and can hardly form more than a thousandth part of the entire text." (*The New Testament in the Original Greek*, II, p. 2). Since Hort's day, many have latched on to this and made the further claim that these differences could be contained on one page.

Note a recent example:

> To put this "thousandth part of the entire text" into perspective, I am looking at the last page of my Greek New Testament. It is numbered 895. Hort's estimate means that if all of the substantial variation between the families was grouped together in one place it would combine to occupy less than one page of my entire Testament. (Mark Minnick, "Let's Meet the Manuscripts," *From the Mind of God to the Mind of Man*, pp. 85, 86).

We wonder if those making and repeating this kind of statement really mean to be taken seriously. It is indeed the opposite! The 8000+ differences have a substantial and corrupting effect on the New Testament.

CHAPTER 8

The Theory Behind the Shorter and Altered Text

Are words missing from the modern Bibles or have they been added to the Authorised Version? Where does responsibility lie for the many other variations between the two kinds of Greek text? This is the question that must now be asked! Have words been deleted, either intentionally or accidentally from the text underlying the modern versions, or have they been somehow added to the text of the King James Version?

The roots of the current controversy over the text of the New Testament began with the rise of modernistic theology during the 18th and 19th Centuries. Proponents of the new rationalism gained control within the universities of Europe. This was accompanied by an increasing attack upon the Authorised Version and the Received Text. The moves for revision became such that by the second half of the19th Century a formal decision was made to construct a revised Greek New Testament based primarily on two very old (and disused!) manuscripts.

The Two Old (and Disused!) Manuscripts

The "pillars" of the revised text would be the two famous mid fourth century manuscripts: Vaticanus (B) and Sinaiticus (Aleph). These well-preserved codices contain most of the New Testament as well as the Old Testament in Greek and the Apocrypha. Vaticanus has for centuries been in the Vatican library, while Sinaiticus, was discovered in 1844 in a monastery at the foot of the traditional Mt. Sinai. It can now be seen at the British Library Museum.

Though differing among themselves, they exhibit most of the omissions listed above along with the 8000+ differences when compared with the Received Text. They are the simple reason why the text of the modern versions is shorter. They are corrupted by Adoptionism. They, with partial support from other manuscripts, constitute the basis of the Nestle-Aland and United Bible Society's Greek text.

Manuscripts Aleph and B are continually referred to in the footnotes of modern versions as the "oldest and best manuscripts." They are old but certainly not the best! Their great age and good condition can only point to disuse by the early church. How else could they be in such remarkably good condition? We have no copies made from them in subsequent centuries. The comparatively few manuscripts that also exhibit the shorter text and support some of their readings will often disagree with them in other readings. And, as is well known, Vaticanus and Sinaiticus disagree between themselves over 3000 times in the four Gospels alone.

Their source is Alexandria, Egypt, and their kind of text did not spread and become an accepted text outside of that area. These two primary representatives of the Alexandrian Text remained in their places of disuse for the better part of the Christian era only to be retrieved in the 19th Century to form the basis of the modern Bibles.

Several "Home Truths" About Aleph and B

Given the hatred of the Roman Catholic Church toward the Received Text and toward the great Reformation Bibles based on that text, it would seem surprising that Rome did not in those years use their old manuscript that lay so long in their library as a weapon against what they called the *Paper Pope of the Protestants.* In fact they were very reluctant to let it be examined. During the decades leading up to revision, scholars only with the greatest difficulty were able to gain a complete transcript of its text.

Why? Their prized possession was a *two edged sword,* not only against the Received Text, but also against their own Latin Vulgate, whose text was halfway between the two. Codex B was far too radical of a text even for Rome. It was not until 1975 that Rome gave its official sanction to the Nestle-Aland Text based upon their Vaticanus.

Another surprising point – at least for defenders of the modern versions - is that Sinaiticus unlike Vaticanus contains many corrections and alterations in its margin. Research has shown that a large number of these were carried out shortly after the manuscript's completion. And, the great majority of these revert back to the readings of the Traditional Text.

Nothing approaching an extended direct copy or exemplar of either Aleph or B has been found! The search has been "fruitless", (See T.C. Skeat, "The Codex Sinaiticus, The Codex Vaticanus and Constantine," *Journal of Theological Studies,* 50, pp. 619, 20). In fact Skeat goes on to say that Aleph remained "a pile of loose leaves" for some considerable time, (perhaps as much as two centuries!), before being bound up (p. 609). Early believers wisely ignored these two manuscripts.

For this and other matters concerning early manuscripts see the author's *Early Manuscripts, Church Fathers, and the Authorized Version,* (available from the Bible For Today).

Westcott and Hort: Tailoring the Theory to Aleph and B

In the second half of the 19th Century consensus was reached among those clamouring for change, that the revised Greek text should be based on Aleph and B with preference generally given to B when they disagree. To forward this, at about the time when Darwin was trying to show how there could be life without a Creator, two Cambridge professors, B.F. Westcott and F. J. A. Hort built up an elaborate theory explaining why a shorter and changed text based on Aleph and B should be accepted in place of the Received Text. Their theory received almost immediate acceptance in both conservative and liberal circles. It became dominate and has dominated the field ever since. Few stood against it. The Anglican Dean of Chichester, John Burgon, was a notable exception. Nearly every new translation, both English and Foreign, were now based on the Aleph-B Text. Though the King James Version was to retain its general popularity until the second half of the 20th Century, virtually every conservative Bible College was to use the Aleph-B Text in their Greek departments. Except for Burgon, who was largely ignored, very few took the time to notice that a Trojan Horse had come into their midst, and that the differences this text now introduced where substantial. It was only when the KJV itself began to be replaced in churches that a sustained reaction began to take place.

But, what is so remarkable is that the major tenets of the Westcott and Hort theory have been disproven or diminished by scholars and yet still appealed to by them! It is much the same as with the key theories of Darwin. In the kind of end time day in which we live, it is perversely true, that for many, despite the evidence, they seem no more likely to return to the KJV type of text than an evolutionist whose theories have also been disproven coming back to the Genesis account of creation.

Westcott and Hort and their fellow travellers today have a very big task on their hands. They must explain the dominance and uniformity of the Traditional/KJV Text. The overwhelming majority of known manuscripts fall into this category. In contrast to the Aleph-B Text they are strongly cohesive. How can this be explained? And, what process could account for this vast number of manuscripts being uniformly longer? Here then is Westcott and Hort's attempt at an explanation.

Major Points of the Westcott and Hort Theory

ONE: "In matters of textual criticism the Bible is to be treated like any other ancient book. No special considerations are to be made concerning its claims of inspiration and preservation."

To approach the Scriptures with anything less than the greatest reverence and respect is to reproach its Author! God has committed Himself to His Book in its inspiration, preservation, and transmission. Textual scholars and translators who have not taken this into account have made a fatal error that reveals itself only too readily in the product. As we will see, God declares that His words will be preserved.

TWO: "Conflation or the combining of different text-types (usually the Western and Alexandrian) is the reason for the greater length of the Traditional Text. Rather than choose one or the other, both were used. Much of this took the form of an official revision sanctioned by the Byzantine Church probably under the leadership of Lucan, Bishop of Antioch (died 311)."

For example, if a certain passage in one group of manuscripts reads, "Peter walked by the sea", but another "John walked by the sea"; the manuscripts which form the basis of the Received Text merely combined the two, "Peter and John walked by the sea." This has been the standard explanation for the Received Text's greater length. But, as is now known, conflation cannot begin to account for this, and today textual scholars are reticent to appeal to it.

If it were true, then most of the underlined KJV passages in our lists should be combinations of material from other existing text types. Yet a search of the Alexandrian and so-called Western texts in these passages reveals that there is rarely enough material to be combined. This explains why Westcott and Hort, who were long on theory but short on demonstration, presented only eight (not very convincing) "examples" of conflation. To make conflation the reason for the greater length of the KJV would require virtually thousands of clear instances.

Coming to the second part of the argument, that this conflating was officially carried out around the year 300, history has left not the slightest trace. This historical blank has led modern scholars to speak of the "lengthening" of the Received Text in terms of a "process that occurred over a considerable time, possibly centuries." Yet how such a process unnoticed by history carried out by many scribes, over centuries, across a wide geographic area, could achieve the widespread uniformity so apparent in the Received Text manuscripts is beyond imagination.

THREE: "Despite its numerical advantage, the Traditional or Byzantine Text (as it is called) is merely one of three or four competing text types."

This was the great "leveller" used by textual critics when faced with the overwhelming numbers of the Traditional Text. Rather than view manuscripts on a 90 to 10 ratio (remembering that the 10% though mixed will usually give greater support to the Received Text), the Received Text was made merely one of several competing families. The others are said to be the Alexandrian, Western and possibly the Caesarean. Thus rather than nine to one, the Traditional Text was merely one of four.

For a start, to divide ten percent of the remaining and mixed manuscripts among three textual groupings shows how small each would be. Today it is admitted that because of their lack of uniformity the Western and Caesarean can no longer be regarded as distinct text types. This leaves the Traditional and Alexandrian. And, the Alexandrian is very small as the following shows:

124 Papyri Fragments (2nd-6th centuries):

All but about seven are too fragmentary to show clearly which text they support. However, coming as they do from Egypt, they generally display the doctrinally defaced Aleph-B, Alexandrian Text. Nevertheless, in his important work *The Byzantine Text Type and New Testament Textual Criticism*, Harry A. Sturz has shown that there are many places where the papyri goes against Aleph and B and supports the Traditional Text.

280 Uncial or Large-lettered Manuscripts (4th-10th centuries):

Advocates of the Alexandrian Text claim support from only about nine; most of which, excepting Aleph and B, give as much and likely greater support to the Traditional Text. That is: when tested against the 8000+ only a very few uncials will show greater overall support for the Nestle-Aland Text.

2808 Minuscule or Small-lettered Manuscripts (9th-16th centuries):

Supporters of the shorter text are prepared to list about twenty-two for their side. But again, they are mixed and it is doubtful if even one with respect to the 8000+ differences would give greater support to the Nestle-Aland than to the Traditional Text.

2343 Lectionary Manuscripts (9th-16th Centuries):

These are manuscripts that were divided into sections or lessons for services in Greek churches. With very little variation, they are overwhelmingly Traditional Text and give virtually no support to the Alexandrian Text. For this reason they are all but ignored in the apparatus of the Nestle-Aland Greek New Testament.

Thus the Alexandrian manuscripts comprise only a small fraction of the total number of manuscripts discovered, and there is wide variation among the few that do exist. These two facts place them in stark contrast to the great mass of cohesive manuscripts comprising the Received Text. Among manuscripts of reasonable length, we are probably being too generous in allowing them to claim as many as 40 manuscripts for the Alexandrian side. Forty would be less than 1% of the total number of manuscripts (now about 5555).

But, as editors of the Nestle-Aland Text are adept at *making a lot out of little*, it would be interesting to know precisely how many manuscripts they have which will give greater support with respect to the 8000+ differences. They will not be in a hurry to tell us, but it will be a lot less than 1%. We will come back shortly to this *making a lot out of a little*.

There is only one cohesive text type: that which underlies the King James Version. We will press the question: If the shorter Alexandrian Text used in the modern Bibles is the true text, why did the early church prepare so few and widely variant copies?

FOUR: "The numerical preponderance of the Received Text can be explained by a study of the genealogical descent of its manuscripts. If, for example, of ten manuscripts, nine agree against one, but the nine have a common original, the numerical advantage counts for nothing. It is merely one to one."

This was the classic argument Westcott and Hort used to deny the Received Text any preference on the basis of numbers. The argument implies that many of the Received Text manuscripts are but copies of each other or of near ancestors. But note! Westcott and Hort merely theorized on this; they did not present actual data of parent-to-child and ancestral relationships between manuscripts. Research since W/H has shown that the great mass of Received Text manuscripts are not "mimeographed" copies. Very few have a parent-child relationship. Instead, they are individual representatives of lines of transmission that go deep into the past.

FIVE: "The distinctive Received Text readings (i.e. those we have underlined in the lists) are not generally seen before 350 AD. For the most part they are absent from the Greek manuscripts, Versions, and Scripture quotations of the Church Fathers.

Early Manuscripts, Church Fathers, and the Authorised Version demonstrates the falsity of this argument. Our next chapter, "The Manuscript Evidence for the Traditional Text" deals with the question further.

Clearly, Christians through the centuries believed that the longer text was very old, and accurately represented the original for the simple reason that they continually multiplied copies of it. Given the labour involved in copying a manuscript, they would not have undertaken such a task had they suspected that their exemplar might be a secondary, conflated revision. Textual history demonstrates that on the one hand they consistently avoided copying the Aleph-B kind of text and on the other multiplied and widely disseminated the kind of text that underlies the KJV. This is a better demonstration of the age of the Traditional Text than that of a few 1650-year-old Alexandrian relics that knew nothing of the rigors of continual copying.

A constantly used manuscript could not be expected to last more than several centuries at the most. Given the right climate, a manuscript whose only purpose was to occupy shelf space could last indefinitely. There are old Traditional Text manuscripts, but this explains why the very oldest are Alexandrian.

But, regarding Alexandria, all was not lost even there! We mentioned above that a substantial majority of the scribal corrections in Codex Sinaiticus revert back to the Traditional Text. And, though generally doctrinally defaced, there is significant support to be found for the unique AV Text readings in the papyri.

Nearly all of the 280 uncial manuscripts, the 2808 minuscule manuscripts, the 2343 lectionary manuscripts, as well as a substantial majority of the early versions and Scripture quotations from the early Fathers move strongly to the side of the AV Text. This mass of evidence argues for age and the Original Text far more convincingly than the few, hitherto disused relics, of Alexandria.

SIX: "There are no signs of deliberate falsification of the text for doctrinal purposes during the early centuries."

This allowed Hort (the primary mover of the theory) to treat the text of Scriptures as he would any other work of ancient literature (See Point One).

If he admitted that there had been a significant corrupting of the Scriptures, it would have been difficult for him to introduce his other theories of genealogy, conflation, official revision, text types etc. An unpredictable variable would have been introduced which these neatly packaged theories could not have handled. Textual Criticism approaches the history of the Bible much in the same way an evolutionist does the history of the planet: No direct creation, no flood, all has been left to natural processes, no direct intervention of any kind! In the face of widespread testimony of early Church Fathers to the contrary, it is difficult to see how Westcott and Hort could be serious about this point.

Tertullian of Carthage is typical: He accused heretics of tampering with the Scriptures in order to gain support for their special views. Around the year 208 AD he urged these men to compare their copies with those in the cities where the Originals had been sent. Tertullian may actually be referring to the original autographs of the Epistles of Paul, but if not they were certainly first generation copies.

> Run over the apostolic churches, in which the very thrones of the apostles are still pre-eminent in their places, in which their own authentic writings are read. Achaia is very near you, in which you have Corinth. Since you are not far from Macedonia you have Philippi and the Thessalonians. Since you are able to cross to Asia, you get Ephesus. Since, more-over, you are close upon Italy, you have Rome, from which there come even into our hands the very authority of the apostles themselves. (*Prescription Against Heretics*, 36).

When the Living Word, the Lord Jesus Christ, returned to heaven Satan directed his fury against the Written Word. This fact is essential to under-standing the history of the New Testament text. Any theory not taking this into account is totally adrift.

We are faced with the most direct question. Is the longer or the shorter text the offspring of these attempts at corruption? Did the 100-year period when deliberate alteration took place produce the text that more fully presents the Names, Person, and Work of Christ, or, the one that tends to diminish them? Which would be more likely: a believer adding to the Scriptures, or an enemy of the Faith deleting from the Scriptures? Which would be easier and less liable to immediate detection: adding words and phrases or removing them? Which could be more consistently and uniformly done? And, which of these two kinds of text did believers through the centuries feel convinced to be the right one, and demonstrate their conviction by multiplying copies? By now, you probably know the answer!

SEVEN: "The shorter reading is to be preferred. Corruption by addition is much more likely than corruption by omission."

Another classic example of tailoring the clothes to fit Vaticanus and Sinaiticus! As with the other tenets of W/H it has no real in fact. Regarding deliberate alteration, it is far easier to remove a word or passage and get away with it (for a while!), than to add material. When there is no particular attempt to editorialise, constant copying will result in accidental omission far more often than accidental addition. Supporters of the Nestle-Aland Text admit this:

> But these figures suggest strongly that the general tendency during the early period of textual transmission was to omit…Other things being equal one should prefer the longer reading. (James R. Royse, "Scribal Tendencies in the Transmission of the Text," *The Text of the N.T. in Contemporary Research*, Ehrman and Holmes eds., 1995, p. 246).

But apart from the omission of significant words and passages, the modern version text is shorter in another kind of way. It is terser and not as lucid as the Received Text. And, here it betrays itself that it is not the Original Text of the First Century, but rather one that is altered and secondary.

In Biblical times there were two major kinds of Greek dialect: Classical or Attic (the dialect of Athens on the Attica Peninsula), and Hellenistic or Koine. Though terse and compact, Attic was considered the more "elegant" of the two. It was the language of the golden age of Greece, and was in vogue from about 480 to 323 BC. After Alexander the Great, the more simple and explicit Koine (meaning common dialect) began to be spoken, and became the lingua franca of the eastern Mediterranean region until the fourth century AD, when it was superseded by Byzantine Greek.

Importantly for us, Koine was the dialect of the New Testament; a fact which is a remarkable evidence of God's providence. The Attic left too much to the imagination, whereas Koine with its greater fullness could be more precise. It was simple, lucid, plain, and full; yet without the affected pretence of the Attic.

As time passed there were attempts to return to the Attic dialect. The 2nd Century AD was known as the "century of Atticism" when many did revert back to the Attic brevity. And, as it was an occasion for attack against the Scriptures that they were written in the less cultured Koine, a significant number of "Christian" scholars were caught up in this. Signs point to Alexandria being the prime mover in bringing the Scripture text into line with the Attic dialect. The manuscripts associated with that locality, certainly beyond all others, favour the Attic-like terseness.

When Westcott and Hort convinced textual scholarship to revise the New Testament away from the Received Text and toward Vaticanus and Sinaiticus; these implications were not addressed. Classical brevity was to them an attraction. Subsequent research has shown how wrong they were: the shorter, not the longer, is the altered text!

A Preconceived Malice

This then, with a few other arguments of a more secondary nature, is the Westcott and Hort theory that has resulted in the shorter and altered New Testament of our day. These are the standard arguments against the Text of the King James Version. They are not fair. They are not honest. They do not deal with the actual facts of the case. Most of the argument was tailor-made by F. J.A. Hort to support his preconceived malice against the Standard Text.

Ponder what he wrote to a friend in 1851 when only twenty-three years old:

> I had no idea till the last few weeks of the importance of texts, having read so little Greek Testament, and dragged on with the villainous Textus Receptus. Think of that vile Textus Receptus leaning entirely on late manuscripts; it is a blessing there are such early ones (*Life and Letters of Fenton John Anthony Hort*, 1896, Vol. 1, p. 211).

Even granting his misconception about "late manuscripts," what would make a young man call the Text of the Reformation that had brought such light to the world, "villainous and vile"? Regardless, with this opening salvo he launched into a career dedicated to the overthrow of the Received Text.

Ernest Colwell wrote:

> The dead hand of Fenton John Anthony Hort lies heavy upon us. In the early years of this century Kirsopp Lake described Hort's work as a failure, though a glorious one. But Hort did not fail to reach his major goal. He dethroned the Textus Receptus. ("Scribal Habits in Early Papyri," *The Bible in Modern Scholarship*, Abingdon, 1965, p. 370).

To the contrary, God preserved His Words. For many, even in these last days, the King James Bible and the Received Text are well and comfortably enthroned.

CHAPTER 9

Manuscript Evidence for the Traditional Text

1. The Greek Manuscripts: Their Current Number

The liberal Institute for New Testament Textual Research in Munster, Germany, is the home of the Nestle-Aland Text. It also maintains the international recording list for Greek manuscripts of the New Testament. All manuscripts found anew anywhere in the world are recorded and examined by them. Though they list all manuscripts, their only real interest lies with those that depart to some extent from the Traditional Text and give at least partial support to the Aleph and B base of their text. With well over 90% of manuscripts giving strong and consistent support to the Traditional Text, and with most of the rest, though mixed, still giving it greater overall support, the vast majority of manuscripts numbered below are ignored in the Nestle-Aland Text.

As of August 2009, the Institute gave what they called the "nominal" figures for the total number of known manuscripts. Previously, their figures for February 2008 were for some reason higher. Perhaps a number of manuscripts have since been combined.

Papyri	124
Uncials	280
Minuscules	2808
Lectionaries	2343
Total	**5555**

The One Percent Text

We have already shown that among the above manuscripts of reasonable length, the most that can be claimed in giving a fair amount of partial support to the Aleph-B text would be about 40 manuscripts. That is well under 1% of the total. But, if we were to press further and discover how many among these forty give *greater overall support* than the Traditional Text when tested against the 8000+ differences, we would find that many and likely most give more support to text underlying the KJV. This would give the modern version text overall support from a great deal under 1% of the 5555 manuscripts.

However, the editors of the modern version text, like the evolutionist, are very adept at making a lot out of *this* little.

"The Consistently Cited Witnesses": Making a Lot out of a Little

The Introduction to the Nestle-Aland Greek NT presents three lists of manuscripts. Their *first and best list* is what they call "The Consistently Cited Witnesses of the First Order." Each of the twenty-seven books of the New Testament is given its own list of "first order" manuscripts. Therefore, the same manuscript may be "consistently cited" and of the "first order" in one book, but not in another. For example they may cite a manuscript in Matthew but not in Acts. If in Matthew it departs from the Traditional Text (perhaps 10% or more) but it does not depart so much in Acts, then it will not be cited in Acts. Each NT book has its own list! A manuscript is only allowed to speak in those books where it falls more into line with Aleph and B. This is how they get a lot out of a little.

The Nestle-Aland cites more of these "first order" manuscripts for Matthew than any other NT book. Notice the numbers of "first order" manuscripts in the Matthew list:

Papyri	(18)
Unicials	42
Minuscules	19
Lectionaries	0

The 42 uncials and 19 minuscules are selected by the Nestle-Aland editors because they show clear departure from the Traditional text. How much? The Institute seems to have set guidelines for inclusion in this favoured group, if in a given NT book a manuscript shows at least 10% departure in a set of selected test passages. (Barbara Aland, Klaus Wachtel, "The Greek Minuscule Manuscripts of the New Testament," *The Text of the N.T. in Contemporary Research*, p.54).

This of course means that a number of these "first order" manuscripts could still show as much as 90% agreement with the Traditional Text. In our *Early Manuscripts, Church Fathers, and the Authorized Version* most of these same 42 uncials and 19 minuscules are tested against 356 doctrinal passages unique to the Traditional Text.

The Papyri (2nd -6th Centuries)

Unlike the uncials and minuscules where a selection is made from the mass of manuscripts for inclusion among "first order" manuscripts, the Nestle-Aland cites every available papyri for each NT book, regardless of age or the kind of text. Eighteen papyri have portions containing Matthew. Eight of these Egyptian papyri had fewer than 10 verses. Six had 10-20 verses. Three had 21-32 verses. The verses are frequently not connected. Only one papyri of more extensive length contained Matthew, P^{45}. While many of the papyri are too fragmentary to give an adequate picture as to how they would vote on the 356 doctrinal passages, the few instances that they are able, is generally on the side of the Aleph-B text. The more extensive P^{45} contained 22 of these doctrinal passages and voted 13-9 against the Traditional Text.

All, though, is not lost for the papyri. Harry A. Sturz in his *The Byzantine Text-Type and New Testament Textual Criticism* lists 320 Received Text readings that oppose the early Alexandrian manuscripts, that are read by the mass of later manuscripts, and that are supported by the early papyri. Sturz demonstrates papyri support for a total of 839 readings that in varying degrees would be classed as "distinctly Byzantine" (his term for the Traditional Text). As the papyri is available for only 30% of the New Testament, existing evidence allows us to reasonably project that the results would be the same for the rest of the New Testament.

For statistics on the other papyri fragments see *Early Manuscripts, Church Fathers, and the Authorised Version*.

The Uncials (4th -10th Centuries)

In *Early Manuscripts* the uncials were also tested against their alignments with Vaticanus as opposed to the Traditional text. Here: Manuscripts A, C, D-05 and D-06 gave greater support to the Traditional Text; while Aleph gave more to Vaticanus. Aleph's scribal corrections on the other hand favoured the Traditional Text by 473-181. When the 42 "first order" uncials containing Matthew are tested against the 356 doctrinal passages over the entire NT, only 13 were found to give greater support to the Nestle-Aland Text.

This, I think, gives a reasonable picture regarding overall uncial support for their side. It is not likely that they could claim many more than 13 manuscripts from among the 280 uncials. We concluded that the uncials strongly support the AV Text.

The Minuscules (9th -16th Centuries)

With a total of 2808 minuscules, Nestle-Aland's 19 "first order" minuscules fare badly for their side. Eighteen are combined in two groups that have long been prized by critical editors as showing some departure from the Traditional Text. They are known as Family 1 and Family 13. Tested against the 356 doctrinal passages, the five manuscripts of Family 1 supports the Traditional Text by 100 – 61, and the thirteen of Family 13 by 151 – 21. The one additional manuscript, their "most prized" minuscule is number 33, called the "Queen of the Cursives." In the Gospels it moves closer to Vaticanus, something entirely unique for a minuscule. In the rest of the NT "it looses its crown" and moves back toward the Traditional Text. The 2808 minuscules therefore give nearly unanimous support to the AV Text.

The Lectionaries (9th -16th Centuries)

Though four are mentioned of the "second order," no lectionary manuscripts of the "first order" are listed in the Nestle-Aland Introduction. The 2343 lectionaries give unanimous support to the AV Text. We will see shortly that in a remarkable way they demonstrate the early age of the Traditional Text.

When these details of the Greek manuscripts are analyzed and digested, it can readily be seen that the Nestle-Aland Text of the modern versions is indeed *the 1% Text*.

2. The Early Versions

The early versions, i.e. where Greek was translated into another language, strongly support the Received Text, both before and after 350 AD. The three primary versions are the Old Latin, Syriac Peshitta, and Egyptian Coptic. The two former were translated about 150 A.D. and the Coptic about 200 AD. As might be expected existing manuscripts of the Coptic lean toward the Alexandrian-shorter text. Yet, in a significant number of places the Coptic is found to agree with the Received Text against Vaticanus and Sinaiticus.

The Old Latin

We believe the correct view of the origin of the Old Latin is that missionaries to the Western Roman Empire had translated it in Antioch, Syria. Support for this view is demonstrated by the strong Syrian and Aramaic tendencies in the existing manuscripts. If this is the case then the Old Latin is associated with that city which was not only the missionary center in the Book of Acts, but also the place that history accords as the fountainhead of the Received Text.

The 67 or so existing manuscripts often disagree among themselves and are probably not very good reflections of the original Old Latin text. Those associated with North Africa show some strange additions as well as subtractions. Whereas, the manuscripts connected with Europe are generally favourable to the Received text. The African strain of the old Latin is has been termed "the Western text type." One thing is certain; the Old Latin whether European or African does not give much support to the Alexandrian-modern version text!

It is the branch of the Old Latin used in northern Italy that attracts our interest most, and establishes one of the crucial chapters in Bible transmission history. This version, known as the Itala, is associated with the Christians of the Vaudois - the valleys of northern Italy and southern France. These noble believers withstood every attempt of Rome to "bring them into the fold." From the days of Pope Sylvester (early 300's) unto the massacres of 1655, they were slaughtered, their name slandered, and their records destroyed; yet they remained true to the Scriptures. They are known by a number of names, but chiefly as the Waldensians. Research into the text and history of the Waldensian Bible has shown that it is a lineal descendant of the Old Latin Itala. In other words, the Itala has come down to us in the Waldensian form, and is firmly in the Received Text tradition. The same can be said of other Bibles belonging to those groups who remained separate from Rome. Thus, in the Received Text we have the convergence of the Greek-speaking East and the non Catholic Latin-speaking West.

The Syriac Peshitta

Coming now to the third primary version, the Syriac Peshitta, we have a clear case of textual history being rewritten. From the days of Westcott and Hort and the establishing of Vaticanus and Sinaiticus as the basis of the new Bibles, every attempt has been made to discredit all pre 350 AD evidence for the Traditional Text. This is nowhere more apparent than with the famous Syriac Peshitta.

The importance of this version and the church it came from cannot be overstated. The virtual center of First Century Christianity was Antioch in Syria. "The disciples were called Christians first in Antioch" (Acts 11:20). Paul's great church planting ministries had their base in Antioch. Syrian Christianity had a close proximity and linkage with many of the churches that had received the inspired New Testament letters. The Syrian church had direct contact with the Apostles and writers of the Scriptures, therefore, the Syrian version may have been written with direct access to the original autographs. Indeed, Bishop Ellicott in 1870 wrote, "It is no stretch of imagination to suppose that portions of the Peshitta might have been in the hands of St. John."

During the years following 1870 the good bishop must have bit his tongue for so openly stating this commonly held view concerning the Peshitta's near apostolic age. For in the movement to bring out a revised Bible, in which he himself played a leading role, the Peshitta posed a major stumbling block. Its manuscripts (numbering about 300) are in line with the Received Text! Thus, practically by itself, the Peshitta could undermine the entire Westcott and Hort superstructure.

Their answer was to take two other Syriac manuscripts (one discovered in 1842, the other in 1892), which differed from the Peshitta, and call them the "Old Syriac." The Peshitta was then made to be a revision of this so-called Old Syriac. To complete the rewriting of the history, the Peshitta's date was moved from 150 to about 425 AD, with its "revision" being performed by a certain Rabbula, Bishop of Edessa in Syria.

There is not a trace in Syrian ecclesiastical history of such a thing happening! As Arthur Voobus writes "this kind of reconstruction of textual history is pure fiction without a shred of evidence to support it" (*Early Versions of the New Testament*, pp. 90-97). Further, the view is contrary to the established facts of history. In Rabbula's day a massive split occurred in the Syrian Church. The two opposing sides were known as the Nestorians and the Monophysites (led by Rabbula). Yet, both sides regarded the Peshitta as their authoritative Bible. It is impossible to believe that the side bitterly opposed to Rabbula should at the same time embrace unanimously his "revision" of the Scriptures. Further, such a unanimous acceptance by both parties in the early 400's argues powerfully for the Peshitta's early origin.

Regarding the two sole manuscripts of the so-called Old Syrian text, they are not all that close to each other. One denies the virgin birth of Christ in Matthew 1:16. Nor do they lend particularly convincing support to the Alexandrian Text. In fact, they contain a significant number of Received Text readings. They are merely corrupted copies, all but ignored by the Syrian church, yet with the Received Text base still discernible.

The other European versions-the Gothic (350 AD), Armenian (early 400's), and Georgian (mid-400's) follow the Received Text. Even the Ethiopic (400), despite its proximity to Egypt, is basically Received Text. Therefore, in the early versional history, support for the Received Text, in contrast with the Alexandrian Text, is overwhelming. How the entire range of versions vote with regard to the 356 doctrinal test passages can be seen in *Early Manuscripts, Church Fathers, and the Authorized Version.*

In *Early Manuscripts* an investigation is made of five categories of Greek manuscripts and eighteen categories of early versions. A decisive preponderance of evidence is shown for the Traditional Text.

3. The Scripture Quotations of the Early Church Fathers

Westcott and Hort confidently declared that ecclesiastical writers before 350 AD did not quote from the longer type of text. Their confidence rested in part on what is an immediate disadvantage for the Traditional Text. Most early writers (or at least those who's writings exist now) were located near the areas where the shorter text was prevalent (Alexandria), and where most divergences have been noted in the manuscripts - (North Africa and the West).

Here, and in this entire inquiry it cannot be overstated that in early textual history the Traditional Text is most directly associated with those places that were either the senders or recipients of the original New Testament autographs, i.e. Antioch, Asia Minor, Greece, Macedonia. While volumes of theological literature poured out of Alexandria, North Africa and Italy in the west, very little is available for us prior to 350 from the eastern areas. Yet even with this disadvantage, the Received Text can be shown to prevail in the Alexandrian and Western writings of the Fathers.

Toward the end of the 19th Century John Burgon compiled an extensive index of Scripture quotations from the early Church Fathers. In mentioning Burgon we come to the man who so powerfully and eloquently fought against moves in England to replace the Received Text. Attempts have been made to discredit this good man's massive labours. It certainly cannot be done on the basis of his scholarship. After matriculating at Oxford with honours and taking his B.A. and M.A. there, he was to spend most of his adult life at that famous university. Burgon was Fellow of Oriel College, vicar of St. Mary's (the University Church) and Gresham Professor of Divinity. During his last twelve years he was Dean of Chichester. Unlike many of his contemporaries his was a "scholarship on fire." He believed and loved the Bible, and had a great zeal to defend it. While we cannot go along with his high churchmanship, we acknowledge him as a worthy champion of the Faith, and strongly urge the reading of his books (available from the Bible For Today).

Coming now to the index, Burgon cited 4,383 Scripture quotations from 76 writers who died before the year 400 AD. Edward Miller carried on the work after Burgon's death and put the material in a tabulated form showing the times a Church Father witnesses for and against the Received Text. He found the Received Text had the greater support by 2,630 to 1,753 or 3 to 2. Keeping in mind the Alexandrian and Western localities of these 76 Fathers, we have here quite a strong majority for the Received Text. Had the quotations of the Eastern Fathers been available, all indications are that the support would have been quite overwhelming. But the above evidence shows clearly also that while there was a struggle over the text of Scripture in those early centuries, there was a clear winner!

Miller concluded his research with the following challenge:

> As far as the Fathers who died before 400 AD are concerned, the question may now be put and answered. Do they witness to the Traditional Text as existing from the first, or do they not? The results of the evidence, both as regards the quantity and the quality of the testimony, enable us to reply, not only that the Traditional Text was in existence, but that it was predominant during the period under review. Let anyone who disputes this conclusion make out for the Western text, or the Alexandrian, or for the Text of B and Aleph (i.e. Vaticanus, Sinaiticus), a case from the evidence of the Fathers which can equal or surpass that which has been now placed before our reader. (*The Traditional Text*, p. 116).

Regarding the attempt to discredit Burgon's work by saying that later editors "adapted" the Church Father's quotations to the Traditional Text, Edward Hills writes:

> In regard to my references to the Church Fathers, I am sure that if you examine the notes to my King James Defended and my Believing Bible Study, you will see that I have taken care to look up all the Burgon's references in the most modern editions available. During the years 1950-55, I spent many weeks at this task. In fact, the newer German editions of the Church Fathers differ little from those of the 17th and 18th centuries. Certainly not enough to affect Burgon's arguments (Letter from Edward F Hills to Theodore P Letis, February 15, 1980, as quoted in Theodore P Letis, "Edward Freer Hills Contribution to the Revival of the Ecclesiastical text," unpublished M.T.S. Thesis, Emory University, 1987).

In *Early Manuscripts, Church Fathers, and the Authorised Version* the Scripture quotations of the early Fathers were tested against the 356 doctrinal passages unique to the Traditional Text. Here there was a 2.3 to 1 advantage to the Traditional Text against that of Nestle-Aland.

Psalms 119:89 For ever, O LORD, thy word is settled in heaven.

CHAPTER 10

A Recent Counter Argument

To a large extent we are now dealing with expediency rather than an honest evaluation of the evidence. The publishing houses have invested and made huge sums in the modern versions. The NIV outsells the Authorized Version in many places. The major Bible Societies use the shorter text for their foreign language translations. It is entrenched in practically every theological college. Despite a point-by-point demonstration of the weakness of their position, and of whatever is left of the Westcott and Hort theory, there is simply not the will to upset the status quo. Nevertheless, they must be able to offer some reasonable defence. They may merely try to repeat the old arguments, or raise some secondary points; but as far as factual evidence they have very little to offer for their case. Recently they have come up with an argument which, while not offering positive support for the shorter text might appear to give some credence to their position.

Gordon Fee of Gordon-Conwell Theological Seminary has been at the forefront in seeking to dampen down the resurgence of the Received Text. He makes the following point:

> But the question still must be answered: How does one account for its dominance and general uniformity? How did the Byzantine text become dominant?...By the end of the seventh century the Greek NT was being transmitted in a very narrow sector of the church viz., the Greek Orthodox Church with its dominant patriarchate in Constantinople. By the time of Chalcedon (the famous council of 451 AD) Greek is almost unknown in the west, and after Chalcedon the decline of Alexandria and the subsequent rise of Islam narrowed Greek speaking Christendom still further. ("Modern Textual Criticism and the Revival of the Textus Receptus," *Journal of the Evangelical Theological Society*, March 1978, pp. 29, 30).

It is here argued that the reason for the scarcity of Greek manuscripts with the shorter text is due merely to the fact that they are associated with areas which ceased to speak Greek. This has become something of a last ditch defence for the Alexandrian Text in the face of its paucity of manuscript evidence.

The argument is not valid:

- 1. At issue here is the shorter text of Alexandria, not that of the West generally. The argument tends to give an impression that the scarcity of Alexandrian manuscripts is due to Greek usage dying out in the West. Alexandria, of course, is not the West.

- 2. The Alexandrian Text is precisely what the term implies - the local text of Alexandria! There is little evidence that it spread beyond Egypt. It made no impact on the West or East, neither in Greek, Latin, or the other versional languages.

- 3. The Moslem conquest of Alexandria did not take place until 642 AD. And though the Muslims restricted evangelism, they did not attempt to exterminate Christianity, or compel Christians to convert. Nor does there seem to be evidence that the Muslims halted manuscript transmission in the areas they conquered. Therefore, many centuries were available for the Alexandrian Text to proliferate and establish itself. It did not! Not only did it fail to make an impression on the surrounding regions, but if surviving manuscripts are anything to go by, it also lost favour on its own home base. This is demonstrated by the fact that the very few manuscripts which display this kind of text often do so only in a part of their contents. Also, one of its two primary representatives, Sinaiticus, has hundreds of scribal alterations made near the time of its production that move back toward the Traditional Text. And, that by a five to two margin! This argument does not stand.

CHAPTER 11

The *Huge* Disparity Among the *Few* Modern Version Manuscripts

A hugely disproportionate amount of the variation is to be found among the relatively few manuscripts supporting the Aleph-B text. The critical editors, Barbara Aland and Klaus Wachtel admit this:

> The papyri and majuscules are for the most part individual witnesses: despite sharing general tendencies on the forms of their texts, they differ so widely from one another that it is impossible to establish any direct genealogical ties among them. ("The Greek Minuscule Manuscripts of the N.T., *The Text of the N.T. in Contemporary Research*, p.46. Emphasis mine).

If these few cannot agree among themselves, then why do footnotes in modern versions call them "The Best Manuscripts"? As so little of an Aleph-B kind of manuscript is available, clearly early scribes did not think them best. Nor did the scribes of the 8th/9th Centuries think them best when they transferred the text from uncial to minuscule script. Further, as we have said, the manuscripts that were widely copied are known to be strongly cohesive, with narrow variation margins. Their variation is usually just enough to let us know that they are independent productions with long transmissional lines.

Isaiah 30:8 Now go, write it before them in a table, and note it in a book, that it may be for the time to come for ever and ever:

CHAPTER 12

Key Epochs in the Preservation History

Of the New Testament Text

Given that God has promised to preserve His Words, we would expect these Words that were inspired by the Holy Spirit and inscripturated through the Apostles will be the subject of a number of key epochs during the manuscript period and leading up to the time of printing. Among important events that played a providential role, we mention several:

1. The Early Lectionary Period.

Most do not realise the pivotal role this kind of manuscript played in the preservation of the Scriptures. Lectionary manuscripts are those that were divided into sections for readings throughout the year in services of the Greek churches. Some lectionaries have readings (lessons) for only Saturday and Sunday, others for each day of the week. Many have readings from the Gospels, others from the Apostolos (the rest of the NT excluding Revelation), and others contain both. A complete lectionary would contain two parts: the *synaxarion* - following the religious year and beginning with the variable date for Easter; and the *menologion* - covering the civil year and beginning on September 1.

At a time when most would not have their own copies of Scripture, this system allowed for a substantial amount of the NT along with readings from the OT to be read systematically throughout the year. Some 2343 lectionary manuscripts are known to exist (about 270 are in the uncial script), and virtually all support the kind of text underlying the AV. It is for this reason they are all but ignored in the Nestle-Aland apparatus. Current textual studies are only interested in the very few lectionaries showing some minor departure from the Received Text.

While the oldest extant lectionaries go back to about the 9th century, their formatting system is _very old_. The implications this has for the kind of early text the lectionaries had, as the following quotations shows, is a subject which modern textual criticism would prefer to avoid.

Carroll D. Osburn seems to be wrestling with the issue when he writes:

> Precisely when and where these lections became fixed re-
> mains unsettled. Gregory theorized that the Saturday and
> Sunday lessons probably originated in the first half of the
> second century.
>
> How early then are traces of lections detectable? It is evi-
> dent, possibly from the time of Origen, but certainly from
> the time of Epiphanius, Cyril of Alexandria, and John Chry-
> sostom, among others, that having specific Scripture lessons
> for specific days was customary in their localities. Chry-
> sostom indicates frequently that he is commenting on the
> "lesson" for the day. Consequently, Metzger is of the opin-
> ion that "the lectionary system current today in the Ortho-
> dox Church had its origin sometime during the fourth cen-
> tury."
>
> The question, however, is not settled. For his own reasons,
> Burgon saw the matter as settled by A.D. 348. For other
> reasons, some would not like to admit the origin of the lec-
> tionary system prior to A.D. 300, for it then could be said to
> represent the text of the early period.   ("The Greek Lec-
> tionaries of the NT," *The Text of the N.T. in Contemporary
> Research*, pp. 63,64. emphasis mine).

The implication is clear, and Osburn plainly says so in his last sentence. If the formatting is early so also is the text, and both are the same that we see in the Greek church today. There is every likelihood that the lectionary sys-tem placed a kind of preservative fence around the original words of the New Testament. It became a formal means by which early Greek speaking churches kept the words of Scripture pure and untainted. We see the Lord's hand in this.

2. The Changeover from Uncial to Minuscule Script

While there may be earlier minuscules, the earliest to be dated is MS 461 of the year 835. The actual change of script began in the 7th century, and be-came developed in the 8th. The kind of text which was now being copied into the new script was almost in every instance that which we see in the Received Text.

Barbara Aland and Klaus Wachtel are at a loss to explain this:

> Although transferring other ancient Greek literature into the new script involved "en meme temps un travail critique," (at the same time, a work of criticism), this was not the case for the NT, at least in the sense that no attempt was made to base the newer manuscripts on the oldest available form of the text.... ("The Greek Minuscule Manuscripts of the NT," *The Text of the N.T. in Contemporary Research*, p. 44).

This is a key period in manuscript history. The scribes who undertook this laborious and meticulous work were obviously convinced as to what constituted the True Text.

If one is spending so much time on a project they would want to be certain. To them the text to copy was certainly not the Aleph-B kind. Would not their vantage point into the previous textual history more likely give them a clearer view than ours 1200 years later? They knew to avoid the kind of manuscript preferred by Aland and Wachtel. We see God's hand in this.

3. The Printing and Spread of the Received Text

During the 1500s it does not seem to have occurred to any of those so involved to set type for anything other than Greek editions based upon the Traditional Text. No Greek editions approaching an Aleph- B kind of text got within sight of Europe's publishing houses. There was no debate, no doubt. They knew of manuscripts with aberrant readings and they left them where they lay. The Received Text and the great Reformation Bibles spread across Europe and then to the ends of the earth. Debate, dissent and opposition would come later, but first the pure and full Scriptures were allowed to do their work. With the invention of printing it was this kind of Greek text that would be the first to speak. We see the hand of God in this.

4. The Refining of Printed Editions of the Received Text

The different editions of the Received Text represent the vast majority of Greek and versional manuscripts. Therefore whether it was the editions of the Elzevir brothers (1624,33,41) which were popular on the Continent, or those of Robert Stephanus (1546,49,50,51), accepted as the standard in English speaking countries, the Received Text was the Text *received* by common consent around the world, and represents the Traditional Text of the New Testament. The different editions of the Received Text are not carbon copies; they have slight differences. These differences demonstrate that they are to a certain extent independent witnesses to the Traditional Text.

The Traditional Text in its printed form began with the five editions of Erasmus (1516,19,22,27,35). This paved the way for nearly a century of textual preparation leading to the publication of the King James Bible.

Below are some of the key editions leading up to the translation of the King James Version.

- 1. Erasmus' 1519 edition provided the basis for Luther's German translation. William Tyndale followed Erasmus' 1519 and 1522 editions.

- 2. Erasmus' 1527,35 editions contained some changes from the Complutensian Polyglot (1514). The Complutensian contained the Received Text and the Latin Vulgate in parallel columns. Though prepared by the Catholic Cardinal, Ximenes, its Received Text was very close to the other editions. Rome's Vaticanus manuscript had no effect on its preparation.

- 3. Simon Colinaeus (1534) published an edition based on Erasmus and the Complutensian.

- 4. Robert Stephanus, the stepson of Colinaeus, published four editions (1546,49,50,51). His edition of 1550, known as the "Royal Edition" followed the text of Erasmus' 1527 and 1535 editions. The 1550 also contained marginal readings from the Complutensian. Stephanus' 1551 Geneva edition reprinted the 1550 text and inserted for the first time the current verse divisions.

- 5. In Geneva, Theodore Beza published a total of ten folio (large page) and octavo (small page) editions. After a Latin translation (1556), his four folio editions (1565,82,88,98) became especially influential. These were based on the Stephanus 1550,51 with some changes and notes. Beza's last two octavo editions were published in 1590 and 1604, and his 1565 edition was the primary base for the later editions of the Elzevir brothers.

Of Beza's 1598 edition, F.H.A.Scrivener says:

> Between 1598 and 1611 no important editions appeared; so that Beza's fifth and last text of 1598 was more likely than any other to be in the hands of the King James revisers, and to be accepted by them as the best standard within their reach. It is moreover found on comparison to agree more closely with the Authorised Version than any other Greek text. (*Scrivener's Annotated Greek New Testament*, the Bible For Today, pp. vii-viii).

Regarding places where the AV does not follow Beza, Scrivener further reports:

> All variations from Beza's text of 1598, in number about 190, are set down in an Appendix at the end of the volume, together with the authorities on which they respectively rest. (p. ix).

These 190 differences for the entire New Testament, many of which are very small, are a striking demonstration of the narrow limits of variation within the Received Text tradition. There is, in fact, just enough variation to show the *independence* of the witnesses. Their work reflects a refining process in the providential preservation of the Word of God. Compare this with the many thousands of differences among manuscripts used to support the Nestle-Aland Text.

Scrivener revised Beza's edition of 1598 to the Authorised Version. It was first published in 1881 as *The New Testament in Greek According to the Text Followed in the Authorised Version,* and is the edition most in use today.

The God-consciousness and reverence for the Scriptures of these early Received Text editors is in contrast to the unbelief and rationalism, which characterises nearly all the editors of the critical text.

Edward F. Hills explains how a belief in the Bible's preservation marked the labours of Erasmus, Stephanus and Beza:

> But in their actual editing and printing of the New Testament they were guided by the common faith in the Received Text. For in their appeal to the New Testament against the errors of the papacy and the Roman Catholic doctrinal system these Reformers were not introducing a novelty but were falling back on a principle which long before the Ref-

ormation had been acknowledged by everyone. For centuries it had been commonly believed that the currently received New Testament text, primarily the Greek text and secondarily the Latin text, was the True New Testament Text which had been preserved by God's special providence. It was out of this common faith, therefore, that the printed Textus Receptus was born through the editorial labours of Erasmus and his successors under the guiding hand of God. (*The King James Version Defended*, pp. 62, 63).

We see the hand of God in the refinement of the printed editions of the Traditional Text.

5. Seven Great "Preparatory" English Bibles

The Authorised Version was the culmination of nearly 100 years of preparation. There was intensive study of the Greek and Hebrew Text. The five Greek editions of Erasmus, the four of Stephanus, the nine of Beza provided the translators with a refined representative of the Traditional Text which was in the majority of manuscripts, and had been acknowledged (John 16:13) by God's people through the centuries. There were no fewer than seven "preparatory" English translations: Tyndale, Coverdale, Matthews, Great, Taverners, Geneva, and Bishops. The fifty or so AV translators were men of unparalleled scholarship, representing the combined intellectual might of Oxford and Cambridge. But far more importantly, they were marked by a holy awe and deep reverence for the Word of God. It is this latter, and an insight into which we will see shortly, that places them poles apart from the translating teams of today.

6. The King James Version: A Four Hundred Year Standard

In the translation of the Authorised Version we have one of the great epochs in the history of Scripture preservation. God's Words, which had been providentially watched over, were now to be brought into a *primary* and *standard* translation ("one principle good one, not justly to be excepted against," *The Translators to the Reader*, XV:2) in a language that would be a *world* language. The fifty greatest scholars of the time, who *sought Him that hath the key of David* (XV:8) knew where to find the Words which in the beginning *holy men of God spake as they were moved by the Holy Ghost.* They knew which manuscripts, which versions, which Fathers preserved these inspired Words. They knew to avoid the corrupted texts, which according to II Corinthians 2:17 were *many.*

In their scholarly diligence, and above all, their devotion to the Scriptures, they knew how to translate these Words. An insight as to the nature of how they approached their work can be seen below in the key extracts from *The Translators to the Reader.* Relying upon God, and with the greatest care, these sacred Words were placed in the bosom of the English language at a time when that language was best able to receive them.

No labour was spared, as *they brought back to the anvil that which they had hammered* (XV:20). The translation was fully accurate and intact. It was word for word expressive of the original inspired Words: reverent, exhortative, convicting, meditative, comforting, timeless. Though now in English, "the King's speech remained the King's speech."

7. The Traditional Text Kept Separate from the Modern Versions!

This may at first seem like a strange argument for the preservation of the New Testament Text. But God, it would seem, has prevented His Inspired, Preserved and Uncorrupted Words from being the base of an endless succession of inferior translations. The Traditional Text had been and should remain, the domain of those translators who honour Him. Let today's liberal, new evangelical, "dynamic equivalence" kind of translator have their Nestle-Aland Text. The Received Text belongs solely to Godly translators who do not lessen, weaken and corrupt the Scriptures.

This raises a question concerning the New King James Version, which appears to be an exception to the above as it purports to be based on the Received Text. It is based on the Received Text, but the story does not end there. Nine of the translators who were involved with the NIV took part in the translation of the NKJV. Thus a common philosophy will in part extend to both translations. It is based on the Received Text, but also departs from it in a number of places. Its introduction, while saying some good things, seeks to minimize the differences between the different types of manuscripts; including the large omissions in Mark 16 and John 8.

The NKJV undermines faith in the Received Text by continual footnotes referring the reader to the alternatives of the Nestle-Aland Text, and also another edition that has misleadingly been called the *Majority Text.* (See the authors *When the KJV Departs From the So-Called Majority Text*). While it claims to be a revision of the KJV, it is in reality a new translation, and as research has shown, an inferior one. It is more difficult to memorize, and does not appear to be memorized any more than the other modern versions. It does not have the cadence, the declarative force, the devotional quality of the KJV. Without formal notice literally thousands of changes have been made to the NKJV over the years since its inception in 1979. The NKJV is a door opener to the other modern Bibles and their corrupted text. It is not a safe Bible for the Christian.

Coming back to our point, the issue is much clearer when we realise that nearly every modern version is based on the Nestle-Aland Text. *They were meant for each other, and they can have each other*! This has kept the Traditional Text separate and apart from inferior and unworthy translating practices. We can see the hand of God in this.

CHAPTER 13

Antioch or Alexandria

There is one point upon which both sides of the current debate agree: the early history of the New Testament Text is a "tale of two cities," Antioch and Alexandria. And, just as surely as the KJV Text was woven into the spiritual life of Antioch in Syria, so was also the modern version text among the "scholarship" of Alexandria. Today a believer must decide whether he is more comfortable with a Bible whose roots go back to one or the other of these two cities. The choice is a clear one, as there is very little common ground between them.

Certainly Antioch has by far the greater Biblical heritage. It became to the Gentile Christians what Jerusalem had been to the Jews, and superseded Jerusalem as the base for the spread of the Gospel. The "disciples were called Christians first in Antioch" (Acts 11:26). It was the starting point for the Apostle Paul's missionary journeys. Mark, Barnabas, and Silas were there. Peter and probably Luke were there. The Book of Acts presents Antioch as the center of early church activity.

Egypt shares no such heritage. Biblically it pictures the world, and the world in its opposition to the things of God. God would not allow His Son (Mt. 2), His nation (Ex. 12), His patriarchs (Gen. 50), or even the bones of the patriarchs (Ex. 13:19) to remain there. The Jews were warned repeatedly not to return to Egypt. Not to rely upon it for help. Not to even purchase horses there, etc. Thus, in contrast to what is being claimed today, it is hard to believe that Egypt and Alexandria would have been the central place where God would preserve His Holy Word. Frankly, it was the last place on earth that one could trust in doctrinal and Biblical matters. It certainly wasn't safe to get a Bible there!

Even the late Bruce Metzger, a fervent supporter of the Alexandrian Text, was compelled to catalogue the vast amount of religious corruption that came from Alexandria:

> Among Christians which during the second century either
> originated in Egypt or circulated there among both the or-
> thodox and the Gnostics are numerous apocryphal gospels,
> acts, epistles, and apocalypses. Some of the more notewor-
> thy are the Gospel according to the Egyptians, the Gospel of
> Truth, the Gospel of Thomas, the Gospel of Philip, the
> Kerygma of Peter, the Acts of John, the Epistle of Barnabas,

the Epistle of the Apostles, and the Apocalypse of Peter. There are also fragments of exegetical and dogmatic works composed by Alexandrian Christians, chiefly Gnostics during the second century. We know, for example, of such teachers as Basilides and his son Isidore, and of Valentinus, Ptolemaeus, Heracleon, and Pantaenus. All but the last-mentioned were unorthodox in one respect or another. In fact, to judge by the comments made by Clement of Alexandria, almost every deviant Christian sect was represented in Egypt during the second century; Clement mentions the Valentinians, the Basilidians, the Marcionites, the Peratae, the Encratites, the Docetists, the Haimetites, the Cainites, the Ophites, the Simonians, and the Eutychites. What proportion of Christians in Egypt during the second century were orthodox is not known. (*The Early Versions of the New Testament*, Clarendon Press, p. 101).

Let it be said again: Alexandria was the worst possible place to go for a Bible! Yet it is precisely the place that our present-day translators have gone in gathering Aleph, B, and the papyri as sources for their modern versions.

CHAPTER 14

Timeless or Time-bound

Translators of the Authorised Version and the other great Bibles believed that the Scriptures unfold absolute truth which transcended time and culture. Though the events and discourses of Scripture take place in a past age, and in a civilization different from our own; by the working of the Holy Spirit it speaks directly to the heart in all cultures and times. That this is so is demonstrated by man's common union in the fall of Adam (Rom. 5:12) and his need of the One Saviour (Acts 4:12). This two-fold unity overrides any considerations of time and culture.

There may have been the need for certain normal adjustments, but there was never a question of translating the Bible any other way than the way God gave it. It was also acknowledged by translators that there were many deep things in the Bible which could not be translated simply enough for "modern man" to understand at first reading. Any such attempt would "translate away the meaning"! Therefore, this idea of bringing the Bible "down to the people" had definite limits.

With the advent of Eugene A. Nida and his widely accepted "Dynamic Equivalence Theory" this has all changed. According to him the message and events of Scripture are "bound in their ancient time and culture." By merely using the "static" equivalence method of translation, i.e. word for word translation, the message of the Bible remains bound as far as modern man is concerned. But when the principles of "dynamic" equivalence are applied the message will naturally "leap out" at him into his own day and surroundings; or so Nida would like us to think.

Nida says that formerly there was a one-sided regard for the message, but today the emphasis should be on how the message is connected with its receptor (the certain people to whom the message is sent). Thus, the translator must consider more than just the differences between two languages; he must consider the cultural differences and the differences between the past and present. If (to use one of Nida's example) the people of Jacob's day understood his wrestling with the angel in a literal sense, the people of this day probably would not. Therefore, the translator should, to a certain extent, adapt and translate Genesis 32 "psychoanalytically or mythologically."

It becomes apparent that so long as the translator "gets the message across," this method allows for a great deal of liberty to be taken with the events and discourses of Scripture.

Speaking in irony of this new method, missionary director Dan Truax writes:

> Admittedly, the readers in the jungles of Brazil would understand Isaiah 1:18 better with the "corn flour" substitution. The "corn flour translation" would read as follows:
> Though your sins be as scarlet, they shall be as white as corn flour.
> But consider the dilemma of those translators when they came to certain Bible verses into which "flour" in the place of "snow" would not fit.
> He slew a lion in a pit in a corn flour day. (1 Chronicles 11:22).
> For as the rain cometh down and the corn flour from heaven. (Isaiah 55:10).
> What happened to the old practice of translating the Bible as it was, and then explaining concepts that were strange to the readers? (B.I.M.I. World).

There is a limit as to how far the advocates of Dynamic Equivalency will go. Obviously, if the translation becomes too radical it will not be accepted. "The cultural adaptation must not totally enter the translation. At the same time, they are convinced that cultural adaptation is necessary." Therefore, they speak of the church as a "transformer of the truth" which completes the process began by the translator. Thus if the translator cannot convey that Jacob wrestling with the angel was really a "psychological struggle," the church and preacher should make that supposed fact known!

Virtually all recent translations, and the work of the Bible Societies generally, have to a large extent been influenced by Dynamic Equivalence. It has made Eugene Nida the most influential person in the field. The theory is grounded in theological liberalism. It strips the Bible of its doctrinal content. It dishonours God by implying He is unable to speak absolutely to all generations and cultures. And, to quote the verdict that a literary critic gave concerning the New International Version, it makes the Bible "Formica flat."

That the New International Version was influenced by Dynamic Equivalence is demonstrated by the following statement in its Preface:

> Because for most readers today the phrase "the LORD of hosts" and "God of hosts" have little meaning, this version renders them "The LORD Almighty and God Almighty" (p. ix).

Thus, they have confounded LORD of hosts with El Shaddai: (God Almighty)!

It is not only the underlying text that is at fault in the modern versions; the translation itself is seriously defective. Thankfully you'll not have to worry about either when you meditate in the pages of the King James Bible. For an excellent study (to whom I am indebted for the above), see *The Future of the Bible* by Jakob van Bruggen.

The Bible's Final Warning

Tampering with the Bible is more than academic wrangling; it has eternal implications. The Bible warns against this many times (Deut. 4:2; Prov. 30:6; Jer. 26:2). The Bible's Final Warning is clear:

> *For I testify unto every man that heareth the words of the prophecy of this book, If any man shall add unto these things, God shall add unto him the plagues that are written in this book: And if any man shall take away from the words of the book of this prophecy, God shall take away his part out of the book of life, and out of the holy city, and from the things which are written in this book. (Revelation 22:18, 19).*

This warning in the first instance refers to the Book of Revelation. But, it is the Book of Revelation in its position as the <u>Conclusion of Scripture</u>. It is a warning for the entire Bible. This is evident, as warnings of this kind are not found at the end of any of the other sixty-five books of Scripture. That modern Bible translators do not take this warning seriously does not diminish its force and fulfilment.

Psalms 100:5 For the LORD is good; his mercy is everlasting; and his truth endureth to all generations.

CHAPTER 15

AV Or NIV English

With the advent of the Internet and its effect on global business, the English language itself has become globalised on an ever-increasing scale. It has been a primary medium through which the Word of God has spread during these last centuries of church history. And, in these final days before Christ returns, this globalisation of English is an important aid in the carrying out of the Great Commission. There are however a number of reasons why the AV and its English remains better suited as a vehicle for divine revelation in these last days.

While the AV English is *different*, it is not *difficult*. It is an evidence of God's providence that after four centuries, so little can be found to be archaic to the point of not being understood. Certainly there is a big difference between the Elizabethan English of that day and current English. The AV, however, is not Elizabethan English! As a comparison will show, there is a great difference between AV English and the wordy, affectatious Elizabethan style.

Far from our Bible being a product of that day's literary style, the English language after 1611 owes its development to the Authorized Version! "The King James Version was a landmark in the development of English prose. Its elegant yet natural style had enormous influence on English-speaking writers." (World Book Encyclopedia). This partially explains why the AV is ever fresh and lucid while most else from that period is very difficult to read.

Edward Hills speaks on the misconception that the English of the AV is Elizabethan:

> The English of the King James Version is not the English of the early 17th century. To be exact, <u>it is not a type of English that was ever spoken anywhere</u>. It is biblical English, which was not used on ordinary occasions even by the translators who produced the King James Version. As H. Wheeler Robinson (1940) pointed out, one need only compare the preface written by the translators with the text of their translation to feel the difference in style. And the observations of W.A. Irwin (1952) are to the same purport. The King James Version, he reminds us, owes its merit, not to 17th-century English - which was very difficult - but to its faithful translation of the original. Its style is that of the

Hebrew and of the New Testament Greek. Even in their use of thee and thou, the translators were not following 17th-century English usage but biblical usage, for at the time these translators were doing their work these singular forms had already been replaced by the plural you in polite conversation. (*The King James Version Defended*, pp. 218, emphasis mine).

In 1604 when James I authorised preparations for a new English version of the Bible, a watershed was reached not only in the history of Bible translation, but of the history of the English language itself.

CHAPTER 16

The Translators to the Reader

The Epistle Dedicatory to James I is placed in most editions of the Authorized Version, but the much longer *The Translators to the Reader* is rarely included. This is unfortunate, for it gives unparalleled insights into the nature and work of the Translators. Through their spokesman or spokesmen, we have here what they themselves said about this great translating work. It is this that makes the Preface the most important historical document we have concerning the translation of the Authorized Version.

According to Scrivener:

> The reputed author of this noble Preface...is Dr. Miles
> Smith of the first Oxford Company who would naturally be
> one of the six final revisers and became Bishop of Glouce-
> ster in 1612 (*Authorized Version*, p. 39).

The Translators to the Reader reveals a love for Christ and zeal for the Scriptures that places it on a level far above what we see in today's translation prefaces. Anyone who takes the time to read and compare it with that of the NASV, NIV or NKJV will see that we have something here that is completely different.

The Preface is not necessarily easy reading, and may seem tedious in places. It is long, and for most too long, a point that is made near its conclusion:

> Many other things we might give thee a warning of gentle
> Reader, if we had not exceeded the measure of a preface al-
> ready (XVIII:1).

Much of it deals with the opposition that the Translators were facing and expecting to face, coupled with the need for translations of the Scriptures generally, and for this translation in particular. Many early writers and church fathers are quoted. There is therefore a great deal of material, which while important for presenting the arguments at that time, may in fact distract the reader from coming to grips with those things that are most important for us today. In this presentation, we have what I think are the key statements, and which should give considerable help to those who stand for the King James Bible today.

The Preface is available online. The best presentation is the one formatted by A.V. Bible Tracts and Books.

In addition to other helps, they have divided the Preface's 18 titled sections into 272 numbered sub-sections. This makes the document much easier
to reference and was an aid in identifying the most important statements. Below are 56 taken from among the 18 headings.

I The best things have been calumniated 1-11.

II Anacharsis with others 1-14.

III The highest personages have been calumniated 1-12.

IV His Majesty's constancy, notwithstanding calumniation, for the survey of
the English translations 1-6.

V The Praise of the Holy Scriptures 1-27 (19, 22-27).

• 19 The Scriptures then being acknowledged to be so full and so perfect, how
can we excuse ourselves of negligence, if we do not study them? of curiosity,
if we be not content with them?

• 22 It is not only an armour, but also a whole armoury of weapons, both of-
fensive and defensive; whereby we may save ourselves and put the enemy to
flight.
• 23 It is not an herb, but a tree, or rather a whole paradise of trees of life,
which bring forth fruit every month, and the fruit thereof is for meat, and the
leaves for medicine.
• 24 It is not a pot of *Manna*, or a cruse of oil, which were for memory only,
or for a meal's meat or two, but as it were a shower of heavenly bread sufficient for a whole host, be it never so great; and as it were a whole cellar full of
oil vessels; whereby all our necessities may be provided for and our debts
discharged.
• 25 In a word, it is a panary [bread pantry] of wholesome food, against
fenowed [mouldy] traditions; a physician's shop (Saint *Basil* calleth it) of pre-
servatives against poisoned heresies; a pandect [a complete body] of profitable laws against rebellious sprits; a treasury of most costly jewels against
beggarly rudiments; finally, a fountain of most pure water springing up unto
everlasting life.
• 26 And what marvel? the original thereof being from heaven, not from earth;
the author being God, not man; the inditer, the Holy Spirit, not the wit of the
Apostles or Prophets; the penmen, such as were sanctified from the womb,
and endued with a principal portion of God's Spirit; the matter, verity, piety,

purity, uprightness; the form, God's word, God's testimony, God's oracles, the word of truth, the word of salvation, etc.; the effects, light of understanding, stableness of persuasion, repentance from dead works, newness of life, holiness, peace, joy in the Holy Ghost; lastly, the end and reward of the study thereof, fellowship with the Saints, participation of the heavenly nature, fruition of an inheritance immortal, undefiled, and that never shall fade away.
• 27 Happy is the man that delighteth in the Scripture, and thrice happy that meditateth in it day and night.

VI Translation Necessary   1-9 (1,8,9).

• 1 But how shall men meditate in that, which they cannot understand? How shall they understand that which is kept close in an unknown tongue? as it is written, *Except I know the power of the voice, I shall be to him that speaketh, a Barbarian, and he that speaketh, shall be a Barbarian to me.*

• 8 Translation it is that openeth the window, to let in the light; that breaketh the shell, that we may eat the kernel; that putteth aside the curtain, that we may look into the most holy place; that removeth the cover of the well, that we may come by the water, even as *Jacob* rolled away the stone from the mouth of the well, by which means the flocks of *Laban* were watered.
• 9 Indeed, without translation into the vulgar tongue, the unlearned are but like children at *Jacob's* well (which was deep) without a bucket or something to draw with: or as that person mentioned by *Isaiah*, to whom when a sealed book was delivered, with this motion, *Read this, I pray thee*, he was fain [compelled] to make this answer, *I cannot, for it is sealed.*

VII Translation of the Old Testament out of the Hebrew into Greek 1-27.

VIII Translation out of Hebrew and Greek into Latin   1-4.

IX The translating of the Scripture into the vulgar tongues   1-21.

X The unwillingness of our chief adversaries, that the Scriptures should be divulged in the mother tongue, etc.   1-7.

XI The speeches and reasons, both of our brethren and of our adversaries, against this work   1-11.

XII A Satisfaction To Our Brethren   1-19 (6,7,10,11,12,15,16).

• 6 Yet for all that, as nothing is begun and perfected at the same time, and the later thoughts are thought to be the wiser: so, if we building upon their foundation that went before us, and being holpen by their labours, do endeavour to make that better which they left so good, no man, we are sure, hath cause to mislike us; they, we persuade ourselves, if they were alive, would thank us.

• 7 The vintage of *Abiezer*, that strake the stroke: yet the gleaning of grapes of *Ephraim* was not to be despised. See *Judges 8, verse 2.*

• 10 How many books of profane learning have been gone over again and again, by the same translators, by others? Of one and the same book of *Aristotle's* Ethics, there are extant not so few as six or seven several translations.

• 11 Now, if this cost may be bestowed upon the gourd, which affordeth us a little shade, and which to-day flourisheth but to-morrow is cut down, what may we bestow, nay, what ought we not to bestow, upon the vine, the fruit whereof maketh glad the conscience of man, and the stem whereof abideth for ever?

• 12 And this is the Word of God, which we translate.

• 15 Therefore let no man's eye be evil, because his Majesty's is good; neither let any be grieved that we have a Prince that seeketh the increase of the spiritual wealth of Israel, (let *Sanballats* and *Tobiahs* do so, which therefore do bear their just reproof but let us rather bless God from the ground of our heart, for working this religious care in him to have the translations of the Bible maturely considered of and examined.

• 16 For by this means it cometh to pass, that whatsoever is sound already (and all is sound for substance, in one or other of our editions, and the worst of ours far better than their authentic vulgar) the same will shine as gold more brightly, being rubbed and polished; also, if anything be halting, or superfluous, or not so agreeable to the original, the same may be corrected, and the truth set in place.

XIII An answer to the imputations of our adversaries   1-17 (1,2).

• 1 Now to the latter we answer, that we do not deny, nay, we affirm and avow, that the very meanest translation of the Bible in English, set forth by men of our profession, (for we have seen none of theirs of the whole Bible as yet) containeth the Word of God, nay, is the Word of God.

• 2 As the King's Speech which he uttered in Parliament, being translated into *French, Dutch, Italian,* and *Latin,* is still the King's Speech, though it be not interpreted by every translator with the like grace, nor peradventure so fitly for phrase, nor so expressly for sense, everywhere.

XIV A Third Cavil   1-24 (12,14,20,21).

• 12 But the difference that appeareth between our translations, and our often correcting of them, is the thing that we are specially charged with; let us see therefore whether they themselves be without fault this way, (if it be to be counted a fault, to correct) and whether they be fit men to throw stones at us: *O tandem maior parcas insane minori*; they that are less sound themselves ought not to object infirmities to others.

• 14 But what will they say to this, that Pope *Leo* the Tenth allowed *Erasmus's* translation of the New Testament, so much different from the vulgar, by his apostolic letter and bull? that the same *Leo* exhorted *Pagnine* to translate the whole Bible, and bare whatsoever charges was necessary for the work?

• 20 Nay, further, did not the same *Sixtus* ordain by an inviolable decree, and that with the counsel and consent of his cardinals, that the *Latin* edition of the Old and New Testament, which the Council of *Trent* would have to be authentic, is the same without controversy which he then set forth, being diligently corrected and printed in the printing-house of *Vatican?* Thus *Sixtus* in his preface before his Bible.

• 21 And yet *Clement* the Eighth his immediate successor, publisheth another edition of the Bible, containing in it infinite differences from that of *Sixtus*, (and many of them weighty and material) and yet this must be authentic by all means.

XV The purpose of the Translators, with their number, furniture, care, etc. 1-21 (1-3, 7-21).

• 1 But it is high time to leave them, and to shew in brief what we proposed to ourselves, and what course we held, in this our perusal and survey of the Bible.

• 2 Truly, good Christian reader, we never thought from the beginning that we should need to make a new translation, nor yet to make of a bad one a good one, (for then the imputation of *Sixtus* had been true in some sort, that our people had been fed with gall of dragons instead of wine, with whey instead of milk:) but to make a good one better, or out of many good ones, one principal good one, not justly to be excepted against; that hath been our endeavour, that our mark.

• 3 To that purpose there were many chosen that were greater in other men's eyes than in their own, and that sought the truth rather than their own praise.

• 7 And in what sort did these assemble? In the trust of their own knowledge, or of their sharpness of wit, or deepness of judgement, as it were in an arm of flesh? At no hand.

• 8 They trusted in him that hath the key of *David*, opening, and no man shutting; they prayed to the Lord, the Father of our Lord, to the effect that *S.Augustine* did: *O let thy Scriptures be my pure delight, let me not be de-*

ceived in them, neither let me deceive by them.

• 9 In this confidence and with this devotion, did they assemble together; not too many, lest one should trouble another; and yet many, lest many things haply might escape them.

• 10 If you ask what they had before them, truly it was the *Hebrew* text of the Old Testament, the *Greek* of the New.

• 11 These are the two golden pipes, or rather conduits, where through the olive branches empty themselves into the gold.

• 12 Saint *Augustine* calleth them precedent, or original, tongues; Saint *Hierome*, fountains.

• 13 The same Saint *Hierome* affirmeth, and *Gratian* hath not spared to put it into his decree, That *as the credit of the old books* (he meaneth of the Old Testament) *is to be tried by the Hebrew volumes, so of the New by the Greek tongue*, he meaneth by the original *Greek.*

• 14 If truth be to be tried by these tongues, then whence should a translation be made, but out of them?

• 15 These tongues, therefore, (the Scriptures, we say, in those tongues,) we set before us to translate, being the tongues wherein God was pleased to speak to his Church by his Prophets and Apostles.

• 16 Neither did we run over the work with that posting haste that the *Septuagint* did; if that be true which is reported of them that they finished it in 72 days; neither were we barred or hindered from going over it again, having once done it, like *S.Hierome*, if that be true which himself reporteth, that he could no sooner write anything, but presently it was caught from him, and published, and he could not have leave to mend it:

• 17 neither, to be short, were we the first that fell in hand with translating the Scripture into English, and consequently destitute of former helps, as it is written of *Origen*, that he was the first, in a manner, that put his hand to write commentaries upon the Scriptures, and therefore no marvel if he overshot himself many times.

• 18 None of these things: the work hath not been huddled up in 72 days, but hath cost the workmen, as light as it seemeth, the pains of twice seven times seventy-two days, and more: matters of such weight and consequence are to be speeded with maturity; for in a business of moment a man feareth not the blame of convenient slackness.

• 19 Neither did we think much to consult the translators or commentators, *Chaldee, Hebrew, Syrian, Greek,* or *Latin,* no, nor the *Spanish, French, Italian,* or *Dutch;*

• 20 neither did we disdain to revise that which we had done, and to bring back to the anvil that which we had hammered:

• 21 but having and using as great helps as were needful, and fearing no reproach for slowness, nor coveting praise for expedition, we have at the length, through the good hand of the Lord upon us, brought the work to that pass that you see.

XVI   Reasons moving us to set diversity of senses in the margin, where there is great probability for each   1-14 (1,2,5,6,7).

• 1 Some peradventure would have no variety of senses to be set in the margin, lest the authority of the Scriptures for deciding of controversies by that show of uncertainty should somewhat be shaken.
• 2 But we hold their judgement not to be so sound in this point.

• 5 it hath pleased God in His divine providence here and there to scatter words and sentences of that difficulty and doubtfulness, not in doctrinal points that concern salvation, (for in such it hath been vouched that the Scriptures are plain) but in matters of less moment, that fearfulness would better beseem us than confidence, and if we will resolve, to revolve upon modesty with *S.Augustine*, (though not in this same case altogether, yet upon the same ground) *Melius est dubitare de occultis, quàm litigare de incertis*: it is better to make doubt of those things which are secret, than to strive about those things that are uncertain.
• 6 There be many words in the Scriptures which be never found there but once, (having neither brother nor neighbour, as the *Hebrews* speak) so that we cannot be holpen by conference of places.
• 7 Again, there be many rare names of certain birds, beasts, and precious stones, etc., concerning which the *Hebrews* themselves are so divided among themselves for judgement.....

> [Note: Assuming an AV of 1338 pages, the marginal notes in the first AV edition would average about 5 per page in the Old Testament and just under 2.5 per page in the New Testament. According to Scrivener: of the 767 in the NT, 552 were an alternative translation, 112 a more literal rendering of the Greek than was judged suitable for the text, 35 are explanatory, and 37 relate to various readings almost all of which were derived from Beza's text or notes. Of the 6637 in the OT, 4111 express a more literal rendering of the original (77 of which were from the Aramaic), 2156 were alternative renderings, 240 relate mainly to Hebrew names, and the remaining 67 refer to various readings of the original. (*Authorized Version*, pp. 41,56).

> The marginal notes were in effect a brief commentary showing the breadth of the Original and what it was capable of expressing. In these instances, the translators, who *trusted in*

Him that hath the key of David, made their decision as to the
precise wording of the English text, and the passage of time
has demonstrated that this was the correct decision. JM].

XVII Reasons inducing us not to stand curiously upon an identity of phrasing
1-14 (1-3, 12-14).

• 1 Another thing we think good to admonish thee of, gentle reader, that we
have not tied ourselves to an uniformity of phrasing, or to an identity of
words, as some peradventure would wish that we had done, because they observe that some learned men somewhere have been as exact as they could that
way.
• 2 Truly, that we might not vary from the sense of that which we had translated before, if the word signified the same thing in both places (for there be
some words that be not of the same sense everywhere) we were especially
careful, and made a conscience, according to our duty.
• 3 But that we should express the same notion in the same particular word;
as, for example, if we translate the *Hebrew* or *Greek* word once by *purpose*,
never to call it *intent*; if one where *journeying*, never *travelling*; if one where
think, never *suppose*; if one where *pain*, never *ache*; if one where *joy*, never
gladness, etc.;

• 12 Lastly, we have on the one side avoided the scrupulosity of the Puritans,
who leave the old Ecclesiastical words, and betake them to other, as when
they put *washing* for *Baptism*, and *Congregation* instead of *Church*:
• 13 as also on the other side we have shunned the obscurity of the Papists, in
their *Azimes, Tunike, Rational, Holocausts, Præpuce, Pasche*, and a number
of such like, whereof their late translation is full, and that of purpose to darken
the sense, that since they must needs translate the Bible, yet by the language
thereof it may be kept from being understood.
• 14 But we desire that the Scripture may speak like itself, as in the language
of Canaan, that it may be understood even of the very vulgar.

XVIII Conclusion 1-14 (1-14).

• 1 Many other things we might give thee warning of, gentle reader, if we had
not exceeded the measure of a Preface already.
• 2 It remaineth that we commend thee to God, and to the Spirit of His grace,
which is able to build further than we can ask or think.
• 3 He removeth the scales from our eyes, the vail from our hearts, opening
our wits that we may understand His Word, enlarging our hearts, yea, correcting our affections, that we may love it above gold and silver, yea, that we may
love it to the end.

• 4 Ye are brought unto fountains of living water which ye digged not; do not cast earth into them, with the Philistines, neither prefer broken pits before them, with the wicked Jews.

• 5 Others have laboured, and you may enter into their labours.

• 6 O receive not so great things in vain; O despise not so great salvation!

• 7 Be not like swine to tread under foot so precious things, neither yet like dogs to tear and abuse holy things.

• 8 Say not to our Saviour with the *Gergesites*, Depart out of our coasts; neither yet with *Esau* sell your birthright for a mess of pottage.

• 9 If light be come into the world, love not darkness more than light; if food, if clothing, be offered, go not naked, starve not yourselves.

• 10 Remember the advice of *Nazianzene*, *It is a grievous thing* (or dangerous) *to neglect a great fair, and to seek to make markets afterwards*:

• 11 also the encouragement of *S.Chrysostome*, *It is altogether impossible, that he that is sober (and watchful) should at any time be neglected.*

• 12 Lastly, the admonition and menacing of *S.Augustine*, They *that despise God's will inviting them, shall feel God's will taking vengeance of them.*

• 13 It is a fearful thing to fall into the hands of the living God; but a blessed thing it is, and will bring us to everlasting blessedness in the end, when God speaketh unto us, to hearken; when He setteth His Word before us, to read it; when He stretcheth out His hand and calleth, to answer, Here am I; here we are to do thy will, O God.

• 14 The Lord work a care and conscience in us to know Him and serve Him, that we may be acknowledged of Him at the appearing of our Lord JESUS CHRIST, to whom with the Holy Ghost, be all praise and thanksgiving. Amen.

This kind of testimony is unique in the history of Bible translation.

CHAPTER 17

Principles of Bible Preservation

Verbal inspiration of the Scriptures demands verbal preservation. This is the crux of the matter; does God preserve the Words that He originally inspired? If so, to what extent? Is it merely the concepts and basic message that is kept intact; or does preservation, as inspiration, extend to the words themselves? That the Bible declares both the fact and extent of its preservation is made abundantly clear in the following:

• *Know now that there shall fall unto the earth nothing of the word of the LORD. II Kings 10:10.*

• *The words of the LORD are pure words: as silver tried in a furnace of earth, purified seven times. Thou shalt keep them, O LORD; thou shalt preserve them from this generation for ever. Psalm 12:6, 7.*

• *For the LORD is good, his mercy is everlasting; and his truth endureth to all generations. Psalm 100:5.*

• *For ever, O LORD, thy word is settled in heaven. Psalm 119:89.*

• *Thy word is very pure: therefore thy servant loveth it. Psalm 119:140.*

• *Concerning thy testimonies, I have known of old that thou hast founded them for ever. Psalm 119:152.*

• *Thy word is true from the beginning: and every one of thy righteous judgments endureth for ever. Psalm 119:160.*

• *Every word of God is pure. Proverbs 30:5.*

• *The grass withereth, the flower fadeth: but the word of our God shall stand for ever. Isaiah 40:8.*

• *So shall my word be that goeth forth out of my mouth: it shall not return unto me void, but it shall accomplish that which I please, and it shall prosper in the thing whereto I sent it. Isaiah 55:11.*

• *For verily I say unto you, Till heaven and earth pass, one jot or one tittle shall in no wise pass from the law, till all be fulfilled. Matthew 5:18.*

• *Heaven and earth shall pass away, but my words shall not pass away. Matthew 24:35.*

• *And it is easier for heaven and earth to pass, than one tittle of the law to fail.*
Luke 16:17.

• *The scripture cannot be broken. John 10:35.*

* *Being born again, not of corruptible seed, but of incorruptible, by the word of God, which liveth and abideth for ever. 1 Peter 1:23.*
* *But the word of the Lord endureth for ever. 1 Peter 1:25.*

We have a strange contradiction today; Christians claim to believe what the Bible says about its own inspiration but deny or ignore the equally direct statements concerning preservation. The textual theories inherent in the modern versions must by their nature deny what the Bible says about preservation.

1. The Starting Point of Apostasy

The questioning of the Bible's preservation is the starting point of all other kinds of apostasy. Satan in Genesis 3 did not begin his attack by questioning whether there was a God, or whether God created, or whether the doctrine of the Trinity is true. Nor did it begin with the question of whether God's Word was originally inspired. Apostasy began when Satan asked Eve, "Yea hath God said?" "Eve, are you certain that you presently have a full recollection of what God said?" When doubt was given a bridgehead at this point, the other defences soon fell. The same principles apply today: Has God preserved and kept intact the words He originally inspired or not?

2. Preservation Must Be Approached in an Attitude of Faith

Like all Bible truths, the Scripture's teaching on its own preservation is to be in the first instance accepted by faith. Edward F. Hills in his book, *The King James Version Defended* calls it "the logic of faith." The facts and evidence of such preservation will then follow.

3. Preservation is Grounded in the Eternal Counsels of God

The words of Scripture are rooted in the eternal counsels of God. Though inspired and breathed out on earth *in time*, yet these words were in God's mind from eternity. The words of Scripture therefore are as eternal as God Himself. Are we now to believe that he would let them pass away?

> *For ever, O LORD, thy word is settled in heaven. Psalm 119:89.*

4. Preservation is Brought to Pass Through the Priesthood of Believers

The Old Testament text was preserved by the Aaronic priests and the scribes who grouped around them. "Unto them were committed the oracles of God" (Romans 3:2).

In the New Testament dispensation every believer is a priest under Christ. Hence, the NT Text has been preserved by faithful Christians of every walk of life. "Howbeit, when he, the Spirit of truth is come, he will guide you into all truth" (John 16:13).

It was not the pronouncements of church fathers or counsels that determined the Text and Canon of the New Testament. Rather, the Holy Spirit guided His own into the acceptance of the true Word of God. Such copies proliferated, while defective ones were ignored. To this very day, God raises up humble believers to defend His Words.

5. Preservation Extends to the Actual Words

Inspiration is verbal. It has to do with the actual Words of Scripture. Preservation must also deal with these same actual Words, not merely the general teaching or concepts. This is made clear in the above list of verses. Advocates of the modern versions commonly say: "There is not a single doctrine missing." But, what they fail to tell you is that the words that support and develop these doctrines are frequently missing in their versions. The force of the doctrine *is* diminished. Inspiration and preservation of the Scriptures must *both* be verbal.

6. Preservation is Operative in the Spread of the Scriptures

Preservation has taken place in the diffusion of God's word, not in it being hidden or stored away. Stewart Custer of Bob Jones University in seeking to somehow equate the use of Vaticanus and Sinaiticus with the doctrine of preservation said: "God has preserved His word in the sands of Egypt." (Stated in a debate at Marquette Manor Baptist Church, Chicago, 1984).

To take such a position, would mean that believers have had the wrong text for 1800 years, and it has been only with the advent of two liberal British churchmen, and the retrieval of two disused Alexandrian manuscripts that we now have the true preserved word of God. No! The miracle of preservation was operative while the Scriptures were being disseminated. "The Lord gave the word: great was the company of those that published it" (Psalm 68:11). "Have they not heard? Yes verily, their sound went into all the earth, and their words unto the ends of the world" (Romans 10:18).

7. Preservation of the Original Inspired Words Will Result in Standard Translations Based on These Words

Note again Points 6 and 7 from Chapter XI, *Key Epochs in the Preservation History of the New Testament Text.* It is the original Hebrew and Greek Words that were in the beginning *given* by inspiration. It is the original Hebrew and Greek Words that are preserved across the centuries. If these Words have been prayerfully, faithfully, and accurately translated by Godly translators into another language, then that translation may with full justification be called the Word of God. *It is still the Kings speech,* though now in a different language.

As with the Authorised Version, a translation that has the blessing of God upon it will manifest this by becoming a *Standard.* This will take place over a considerable period of time, and among a large number of people. The Latin Vulgate was not a standard. It was the Bible of the priests, not of the people. The NIV, NASV, NKJV are not standards. You cannot have three standards! In their short lives they have undergone frequent changes and revision. Further, and for example, we expect a standard to be memorized, they are not.

Being a *Standard,* and particularly as in the case of the AV, a 400 Year Standard, is the sign that this is the Word of God in English.

8. Preservation Makes It Possible for Copies of The Scriptures to Still be Called "The Scriptures"

Some may assume that the Bible use of the word "Scripture" primarily refers to the original autographs. This is of course not the case. Virtually every time we see the word, it is the copies or even a translation of the Scriptures that is in view. It refers to the copies of the Scriptures that the people then and there had access to. Notice the following examples:

- *I will shew thee that which is noted in the scripture of truth. Dan. 10:21.*
- *Ye do err, not knowing the scriptures. Matt. 22:29.*
- *This day is this scripture fulfilled in your ears. Luke 4:21.*
- *He expounded unto them in all the scriptures. Luke 24:27.*
- *And while he opened to us the scriptures. Luke 24:32.*
- *That they might understand the scriptures. Luke 24:45.*
- *They believed the scripture, and the word which Jesus had said. Jhn. 2:22.*
- *Search the scriptures. Jhn. 5:39.*
- *The scripture cannot be broken. Jhn. 10:35.*
- *The place of the scripture which he read. Acts 8:32.*
- *And began at the same scripture and preached. Acts 8:35.*
- *Reasoned with them out of the scriptures. Acts 17:2.*
- *That from a child thou hast known the holy scriptures. II Tim. 3:15.*
- *All scripture is given by inspiration of God. II Tim. 3:16.*

Here "the Scriptures" clearly refer to what was at hand, what was current, what they could then actually read and hear. The Biblical usage "the Scriptures" is to a great extent to the copies of the Scriptures. Therefore:

- These copies are holy. II Tim. 3:15; Rom. 1:2.
- These copies are true. Dan. 10:21.
- These copies are not broken. Jhn. 10:35.
- These copies are worthy of belief. Jhn. 2:22.
- The prophecies contained in these copies have been fulfilled to the very letter, while others await fulfilment. Luke 4:21.
- These copies are the very voice of God. This can be illustrated by a comparison of the following: Exodus 9:13-16 with Romans 9:17; Genesis 12:1-3 with Galatians 3:8; Genesis 21:10 with Galatians 4:30.

Here, the fact is established that there is no difference between the Scriptures speaking and God speaking. And as the Scriptures refer to that which is current and available, it follows that our copies are as much the voice of God as the original was.

9. II Timothy 3:15-17 and Preservation:

Past Inspiration - Present Profitability

> *And that from a child thou has known the holy scriptures, which are able to make thee wise unto salvation through faith which is in Christ Jesus. All scripture is given by inspi-*

ration of God, and is profitable for doctrine, for reproof, for correction, for instruction in righteousness: that the man of God may be perfect, throughly furnished unto all good works.

There are some remarkable things about this passage. The words "is given by inspiration of God" are translated from the one Greek word, *theopneustos* (God-breathed), and the words "is profitable" is from *ophelimos*. These two words are joined by the conjunction *kai*. All Scripture (*graphe*) is said to be "God-breathed <u>and</u> profitable". Therefore, while the Scriptures were inspired in the past, their profitability has to do with the present. This grammatical construction <u>inseparably links past inspiration to present profitability</u>. Such could not be the case if God did not providentially preserve the Scriptures.

10. John 16:13 and Preservation: Guidance into All Truth

Howbeit when he, the Spirit of truth, is come, <u>he will guide you into all truth</u>.

God has promised to guide His people into all truth. This guidance is based upon, and relative to the Scriptures that He has inspired: Never apart from them! "Truth" is defined in the next chapter as the Word of God.

Sanctify them through thy truth: <u>thy word is truth</u>. John 17:17.

God's people (at least a number of them) would be guided into all truth concerning the Scriptures <u>to the extent that the Scriptures would be completely preserved</u>.

Through the priesthood of believers, God guided His people into all truth as to the Canon of Scripture. For example they knew that II Peter was to be placed in the Canon whereas the so-called *Epistle of Barnabas* and *Gospel of Thomas* where rejected. He guided them into all truth as to the Text of Scripture. They knew that the Text emanating from Antioch was true, but that from Alexandria was corrupt. They multiplied copies of the former and ignored the latter. He guided them into all truth as to the relatively few variations in the Traditional Text manuscripts, thus providing a sound and refined base when the first printed editions of the Received Text appeared, and when the great Reformation Bibles of Europe began to be translated.

From the time of the inspiration of God's Words to the time of their reception into the great Reformation Bibles and most notably the King James Version, a sufficient number of God's people have been guided into all truth to enable the complete preservation these Words. God used people; believers, for this process.

Since that time, guidance based on the Scriptures continues as to the guarding of God's Words. Every period of history has had its defenders who stood their post by God's *once delivered* Words (Jude 3). Back in Burgon's day when the Westcott and Hort *juggernaut* began to rumble across Europe there were very few. Today there are more. But there will always be a sufficient number, whether in the manuscript period, the early printing time, or these last days, to guard God's Words.

We urge *you* to take your stand for *every word* in the Text and the Translation of the Authorised Version. All indications point to the KJV as the Bible God would have His people use in these last days before the Second Coming of Christ. God has preserved in the Hebrew and Greek Words underlying the King James Version His original work of inspiration. Upon investigation, the AV translation of these Words will be shown to display their fullest expression available in our language. We do not deny that here and there they may need to be explained, but when researched a given word will be shown to be fuller than the modern replacements, and with a much longer and more consistent history in our language. Therefore, if necessary: Explain it, but *do not change it*!

The flower has not faded! The Sword is as sharp as in the day it was first whetted! (Isaiah 40:8; Hebrews 4:12).

John 12:47-48 And if any man hear my words, and believe not, I judge him not: for I came not to judge the world, but to save the world. He that rejecteth me, and receiveth not my words, hath one that judgeth him: the word that I have spoken, the same shall judge him in the last day.

CHAPTER 18

Some Further Arguments Against Our Bible

One does not need to "come down from the wall" of service to Christ and answer every criticism a person may raise against our Bible (Nehemiah 6:3). This is especially true if they are not prepared to do a little study on their own. Here are several common criticisms made against the Traditional Text and AV. Fuller answers are available in other books and also on the Net.

1. Erasmus, the first editor of the printed Received Text, was a Roman Catholic and a humanist.

Erasmus (1466-1536) was of course Catholic as was nearly everyone else at that time. But, at his monastery, he was far more of a continual student with a voracious appetite for knowledge than a priest in the normal sense. Also, it is in this respect rather than in the modern atheistic sense that he was a humanist. Many of his writings were scathing against the Catholic Church. He died among his Protestant friends and was buried in a Protestant cemetery. He had embraced much of the teaching of the Reformation, but had not come out openly in its support by formally leaving the Catholic Church.

Erasmus was acclaimed the greatest intellect of Europe, and became the man of the hour to *initiate* the transfer of the Traditional Text from manuscript to printed form. His Greek editions provided the base for the great Reformation Bibles, and lit the fire for the Reformation itself. Many would like us to concentrate instead on his deficiencies, and have us jump from Erasmus and his 1516 edition directly to the AV of 1611. By this they seek to attach any deficiency in the man and his work to the AV itself. (For a fuller account see Edward Hills, *The Kings James Version Defended*, and also *The Bible Version Question/Answer Database* by David Cloud).

2. Erasmus' first edition was published in haste and with many errors.

Much has been made of the publisher Froben's haste in printing Erasmus' first edition (1516) before the Spanish Cardinal Ximenes' Complutensian Polyglot Bible went to press (which also contained the Received Text). But, as it would turn out, in the following year the Reformation was to begin at Wittenberg, and this first printing of the Greek NT was to become a (in fact, *the*!) major impetus of the Reformation. This is a powerful demonstration of God's providence in the timing of the publication. Most of the errors were corrected in his later editions. (See Hills).

3. Erasmus' edition was based on only a half dozen late manuscripts.

This criticism ignores that Erasmus was conversant with many manuscripts in his searches across Europe. Those that he did have before him at Basel for the 1516 edition can be demonstrated to have been good representatives. (See Hills, p.198). David Cloud in his *The Bible Version Question/Answer Database* has gathered a number of important citations on this question, including the following two:

> For the first edition Erasmus had before him ten manuscripts, four of which he found in England, and five at Basle...The last codex was lent him by John Reuchlin...(and) 'appeared so old to Erasmus that it might have come from the apostolic age'. (Preserved Smith, *Erasmus: A Study of His Life, Ideals, and Place in History*, 1923).

> "If I told what sweat it cost me, no one would believe me." He had collated many Greek manuscripts of the N.T. and was surrounded by all the commentaries and translations. (D'Aubigne, *History of the Reformation of the Sixteenth Century*, vol. 5, p. 157).

4. Erasmus' manuscript of Revelation was lacking in the last six verses (22:16-21), and was supplied by referring to the Latin Vulgate.

Herman Hoskier in his massive, *Concerning the Text of the Apocalypse*, has shown that Erasmus may have had Greek manuscript 2049 (Hoskiers' 141) covering these verses (I 474-77; II 454, 635). But whatever the case, if indeed Erasmus used the Vulgate, in his later editions it was corrected by direct reference to the Greek.

One notable exception is claimed to be 22:19 where the AV/TR reads: *...shall take away his part out of the book of life.* This has fairly substantial support in other sources, but is found in only three Greek manuscripts (296 2049 2067mg.). The variant reading, though supported by the Greek, can hardly be said to make sense: *shall take away his part out of the tree of life.* In *When the KJV Departs from the So-called Majority Text,* and using Hoskier, I have listed support from the manuscripts, versions, and Fathers for eight passages in Revelation 22:15-21.

5. I John 5:7 should not be in the Bible. Erasmus said he would insert it only if someone could show him a Greek manuscript containing the passage, to which a manuscript was hastily prepared for that purpose.

A letter from the Erasmian scholar H. J. de Jonge to Michael Maynard in 1995 puts the matter in a different light. Quoting Erasmus in his dispute with Edward Lee, de Jonge says:

> Erasmus first records that Lee had reproached him with neglect of the manuscripts of I John. Erasmus (according to Lee) had consulted only <u>one</u> manuscript. Erasmus replies that he had "certainly <u>not</u> used only one manuscript, but many copies, first in England, then in Brabant, and finally in

Basle. He cannot accept, therefore, Lee's reproach of negligence and impiety."

"Is it negligence and impiety, if I did not consult manuscripts which were not within my reach? I have at least assembled whatever I could assemble. Let Lee produce a
Greek MS which contains what my edition does not contain
and let him show that that manuscript was within my reach.
Only then can he reproach me with negligence in sacred
matters."

From this passage you can see that Erasmus does not challenge Lee to
produce a manuscript etc. What Erasmus argues is that Lee may only reproach Erasmus with negligence of MSS. if he demonstrates that Erasmus
could have consulted any MS. in which the *Comma Johanneum* figured.
Erasmus does not at all ask for a MS. containing the *Comma Johanneum*. He
denies Lee the right to call him negligent and impious if the latter does not
prove that Erasmus neglected a manuscript to which he had access. (Michael
Maynard, A History of the Debate over I John 5:7,8, p. 383).
Jeffrey Khoo points out:

Yale professor Roland Bainton.... agrees with de Jonge,
furnishing proof from Erasmus' own writing that Erasmus'
inclusion of I John 5:7 was not due to a so-called "promise"
but the fact that he believed "the verse was in the Vulgate
and must therefore have been in the Greek text used by
Jerome." (*Kept Pure in all Ages*, p.88; cited from D.W.
Cloud, *The Bible Version Question/Answer Database*,
p.343). See also *And These Three are One* by Jesse Boyd,
Wake Forest, 1999.

Michael Maynard's monumental work on the disputed passage will, I
think, demonstrate that this has not been a debate over "thin air." His book
chronicles the fact that defence of the faith and defence of this passage frequently went hand in hand. Beginning from the days of Cyprian of Carthage
(died 258), there is indeed substantial evidence for the passage. Cyprian said:

The Lord saith, "I and the Father are one;" and again it is
written concerning the Father, Son and Holy Spirit, "And
three are one". (de Catholicae ecclesiae unitate, c.6).

Critics have argued that Cyprian was merely giving a Trinitarian inter-pretation to verse 8. *The spirit, and the water, and the blood: and these three agree in one.*

The answer to this is obvious; the figures of verse 8 cannot naturally be interpreted as the <u>Persons</u> of the Holy Trinity. (See Hills).

Though missing in most Greek manuscripts, <u>it nevertheless leaves in them its *footprint*</u>! And this, with the mismatched genders that result when the disputed words are removed. The loose ends do not match up grammatically! Native Greek speakers find this "glaring". Here in London, the printed *Apostolos* (the lectionary text used in Greek Orthodox services) contains the passage.

6. The marginal notes in the AV reveal that the Translators viewed their work as being to some extent tentative and provisional.

They reveal nothing of the kind. The Translators viewed their work as being *principle* not provisional.

> Truly, good Christian Reader, we never thought from the beginning that we should need to make a new translation, nor yet to make of a bad one a good one...but to make a good one better, or out of many good ones one principle good one, not justly to be accepted against. (*Translators to the Reader*, XV:2)

History has borne this out, as the AV remains the *one principle good one* after 400 years.

Regarding the marginal notes, these provided a kind of miniature com-mentary. In the comparatively few places where we find them, those transla-tors who *trusted in Him that hath the key of David*, showed by inclusion in the text what their decision had been, while at the same time giving insight into what the Original was capable of expressing. In some cases they demonstrate that a strictly literal rendering into English would have been awkward.

In only 104 instances (Scrivener) is a variant reading from different manuscripts given. Here they show their awareness, but not to the point of distracting the reader, and certainly not to the point as some have claimed that the AV translators would have "welcomed the great manuscript finds that have occurred in the last 150 years".

Erasmus knowledge of variant readings in Codex B is well documented. In an attempt to persuade Erasmus of the superiority of B, 365 variant readings were sent to him in early November 1533 from Rome by the Spaniard Sepulveda (Maynard, pp. 87, 88). Erasmus rejected these for his 1535 edition. They were rejected by succeeding editors of the Received Text, and by the great Reformation Bibles both in English and other languages. The men of the AV knew where the dangers lurked in the manuscript record. For example, Codex D, and the Clementine Vulgate (a much more corrupt 1592 replacement for the Sixtine edition), were at their disposal. They had the spiritual discernment to reject the corrupt variants that these and other sources presented.

7. Many thousands of changes have been made to the AV over the centuries.

Nearly all of the changes made in the Oxford and Cambridge printings of the AV are updated punctuation and spelling, along with correction of some printing errors.

Dr. D. A. Waite's thorough research into this question has shown that very little difference can be detected when reading a 1611 edition and the AV of today. Among the 791,328 words in the AV only 421 showed a *change in sound.* Of these there were only 136 changes of substance, such as an added "of" or "and." (See *Defending the King James* Bible, pp. 3-5, and also BFT 1294). In a recent email to this author, Dr. Waite said:

> "In March of 1985, I wrote a small book which listed the differences that I could hear between the 1611 and the 1769 King James Bibles. To do this, I went from Genesis through Revelation listening with my ears to the recording of the King James Bible while looking with my eyes at the 1611 King James Bible. When I HEARD a difference, I noted it. This is how I found 421 differences to my EARS. These specific differences are noted in my book, *The King James Bible of 1611 Compared to the King James Bible of 1769* (BFT #1294). I did not count spelling differences. There are thousands of these, such as the word, "sinne" (1611) and the word, "sin" (1769). The sound of these two words, however, is identical when read out loud.
>
> In 2006, 21 years after my study was made, a man sent me a study concerning differences between the 1611 and 1769 King James Bibles. Even though his method was entirely different than mine, he scolded me unkindly for my research

by EAR. His study was by the EYE rather than by the EAR. Using this methodology, he claimed to have found some 2,000 differences between the 1611 and the 1769 King James Bibles. He SAW more than I HEARD. When his book arrived, I went through each of the alleged 2,000 differences carefully. I counted only about 1,000 examples that were genuine differences that could be HEARD. Others were either spelling differences rather than difference in sounds, or were not really examples for some other reasons. My purpose in my book (BFT #1294) was to prove that there were relatively few differences to the EAR between these two King James Bibles. Whether the total count of differences in sound is 421, or 1,000, or even 2,000, it is a minute number of differences to the ear when considering that there are 791,328 (almost 800,000) words in the King James Bible. The percentage of differences would be as follows: for 421, only 0.05%; for 1,000, only 0.12%, for 2,000, only 0.25%. I think that all of the readers would agree with me that any of the three percentages is indeed a comparatively tiny number of changes in sound. It is certainly much smaller than some who claim there are over 10,000 changes in sound between the 1611 and the 1769 King James Bibles." (Pastor D. A. Waite, Th.D., Ph.D.)

8. There are too many old-fashioned expressions and words in the Authorised Version.

Actually, after 400 years, there are not! But, we have for example: _Suffer little children to come unto me_; and, _Study to show thyself approved unto God_. These we could replace these with _permit_ and _give diligence_, but the impact would be lessened. We could change _noised_ about to _reported_, but the former gives a better picture of what was actually taking place in Luke 1:65 and Mark 2:1.

Should we not replace the _eth_ and _ith_ verb endings in the AV? Known as the _historical present_ they are there for good reason. They translate a certain usage of the Greek present tense. At times, though the Greek verb is in the present, the action has actually taken place in the past or has past connotations. This was a device in that language to give vividness by bringing a past event more into the present. Therefore if you translate these occurrences with the English present (as the NIV) you will be missing somewhat the sense intended. Or, if like the NASV you use the English past (with an *), you will also be missing the sense. The AV uses the *historical present* (saith, seeth, taketh etc.) as a kind of bridging verb to convey that both the past and present are in view. Therefore while some view the *eth* endings as a distraction, they are a necessity to more accurate translation. (See, *The New King James Bible*, G. W. and D. E. Anderson, Trinitarian Bible Society, pp. 12,13).

We could replace the *thee's* and *thou's* with "you", but would then remove the means of distinguishing between singular (thee, thou), and plural pronouns (ye, you). The Ts are singular, the Ys are plural.

> *Marvel not that I say unto thee (Nicodemus), Ye (everybody) must be born again. John 3:7*
> *And the Lord said, Simon, Simon, behold, Satan hath desired to have you (all the disciples), that he may sift you (all the disciples) as wheat: But I have prayed for thee (Peter), that thy (Peter) faith fail not: and when thou (Peter) art converted, strengthen thy (Peter) brethren. Luke 22:31,32*

Without the distinguishing pronouns, we would think Christ's address was entirely to Peter and not the other disciples. Further, replacing Thee and Thou removes what has historically been the reverent form of address to God.

Among the words termed archaic, I would estimate that not many over 35 or 40 (most are used infrequently) would perhaps need a dictionary. Often, the context indicates the meaning. A study of the history and distinctive meaning of these words will show that they will often have a greater depth of meaning than their modern replacements. It is on reflection, truly astounding, that in comparison with every other 400-year-old book, so little in the AV is archaic. It is a *timeless* Bible.

9. There are translation errors that need to be *strained out* of the Authorised Version.

A classic example of a supposed error of translation in the AV is Matthew 23:24.

> *Ye blind guides, which strain at a gnat, and swallow a camel.*

It should, we are told, be *strain out* a gnat instead of the AV's *strain at*. Wycliffe (1395) had *clensinge a gnatte*, but four Reformation Bibles before the AV (Tyndale, Coverdale, Geneva, Bishops) read *strayne out a gnat*. As subsequent refinements to the AV text allowed this reading to remain, it is highly unlikely, as some have suggested, that this was a printer's error.

The AV translators made a decision to go against their predecessors, and this likely for the following reasons:

(1) The Greek word for *strain* (diulizontes) is found only here in the N.T. It is a present participle (rather than an aorist) and means to strain or filter. The present participle indicates that an ongoing rather than completed action is taking place. It points to the effort involved, rather than that they had succeeded and actually got the gnat *out*. In 1729, Daniel Mace made a translation of the N.T., and rendered the words, *strain for a gnat*, which conveys the same meaning as the AV.

(2) Only one gnat is involved. At first discovery of this tiny, lone, solitary creature all else stopped. Rather than remove it with a spoon, the entire contents must be filtered; suitable cloths were brought, and with much show and ritual the filtering process began. Thus *they strain at a gnat*. That is, at the first sight of only one gnat the filtering ceremony begins.

(3) When "out" is used in the N.T., we expect to see an accompanying Greek preposition, usually *ek* or *apo*. They are not used here. Commentators as Poole, Henry, and Gill (non revised) do not take issue with the AV reading. The AV is correct.

The above is based on www.geocities.com/brandplucked/strain.html

This passage opens up a window into the spiritual and intellectual diligence of the AV translators. It would have been far easier simply to translate the verse as had Tyndale, Coverdale, Geneva and the Bishops, and thereby avoid any further controversy. But they did not, and they translated correctly.

For other passages, see "AV Verses Vindicated" by Ron Smith, waymarks@ntlworld.com Also, among other sources, see the author's *Conies, Brass and Easter*.

It is common today for critics to look for *gnats* in the AV. These are often accepted, when a little homework will show that there is a reasonable and genuinely enlightening solution. The above has been considered one of the strongest proofs of a translation error. We maintain that after 400 years there are no reasonably proven translation errors in our Standard Bible. Given all that can be said in behalf of the AV, the burden of proof must rest with the one making the charge. If they feel they have better understanding and spiritual insight at a given point than did the fifty AV translators - and the translators of the seven propitiatory Bibles from Tyndale to the Bishops - then they must set forth their evidence.

That this is not so easy can be seen from the following incident involving one of the AV translators:

> Dr. Richard Kilby, the translator in the Old Testament group at Oxford, heard a young parson complain in an earnest sermon that a certain passage should read in a way he stated. After the sermon Dr. Kilby took the young man aside and told him that the group had discussed at length not only his proposed reading but thirteen others; only then had they decided on the phrasing as it appeared. (Gustavis S. Paine, The Men Behind the KJV, Baker Book House, pp. 137,8).

A great amount of unnecessary harm has been done by "young parsons" (and older ones!) who do this. Anyone who approaches a so-called problem passage in an attitude of honour towards God's Word will find the solution equally honouring. He will find that God's promise of preservation has been vindicated.

10. Great fundamentalist leaders of the past made favourable comments on the Revised Bibles.

Not until the 1960s and 70s when modern versions began to increasingly displace the KJV, did more concerted and general warnings begin to be heard that a *Trojan Horse* had been brought through the gates. It was late in coming. But, better late than never!

The booklet *Trusted Voices on Translations* (Published by Mount Calvary Baptist Church in Greenville, South Carolina) gathers quotations from many of the great leaders of the past. Here: C.H. Spurgeon, J.C. Ryle, Francis Ridley Havergail, D.L. Moody, Alexander Maclaren, C.I. Scofield, Oswald Chambers, G. Cambell Morgan, Amy Carmichael, H.A. Ironside along with others are heard to make favourable comments on the revised Bibles. But! *No detailed research is mentioned* as coming from these *Trusted Voices*. They merely made favourable statements. No lists by Oswald Chambers are mentioned showing omissions, alterations, missing names of Christ, doctrinal deviations etc. Spurgeon, Moody, Francis Ridley Havergail should have demonstrated from their writings that they had investigated at least some of the many thousands of differences between the two kinds of text, but no indication is given in this publication that they did.

All that *Trusted Voices* can demonstrate is that from Westcott and Hort until more recently many otherwise sound believers <u>did not raise their *voices*</u> when the Westcott and Hort theory raced across Europe and over to America. They should have sounded the alarm but did not. In this their *voices* could not be *trusted*.

Matthew 5:18 For verily I say unto you, Till heaven and earth pass, one jot or one tittle shall in no wise pass from the law, till all be fulfilled.

CHAPTER 19

An Example of the Downward Course that Accompanies Criticism and Rejection of the Authorised Version

This is not an issue that you can put a fence around. You cannot expect that other areas of the Faith will not also be affected. Such an example is Dr. Daniel Wallace, a prominent professor at Dallas Theological Seminary. Dallas, during its earlier days, was typical of many otherwise sound schools: No inconsistency was seen in using the Revised Text in the classroom and the King James Version in the pulpit and private study. Though there were some dissenting voices (i.e. Zane Hodges), this was the common practice, with very little interest shown in the matter. We do owe a debt to the "old" Dallas. In the years following WW II it was at the forefront among institutions in producing a vast amount of material on the Premillennial Return of Christ.

Dr. Wallace, as his website will show, has taken the rhetoric at Dallas against the Traditional Text and AV to a higher level. His short paper *Why I Do Not Think the King James Bible is the Best Translation Available Today* is typical. After giving some of the above arguments, he concludes:

> I trust this brief survey of reasons I have for thinking that the King James Bible is not the best available translation will not be discarded quickly.

For his own good and those who follow him, his reasons should be discarded quickly. It is a downward course. After announcing that he no longer accepts passages as John 3:13; John 7:53- 8:11; I Timothy 3:16, he says:

> I find it difficult to accept intellectually the very passages which I have always embraced emotionally.

Yes, other areas will be affected! The following is from a 9/12/94 article in *Christianity Today* where Wallace praises the neo-orthodox Karl Barth and utters a typically liberal expression in bemoaning *bibliolatry*.

One of the chief legacies Karl Barth left behind was his strong Christocentric focus. It is a shame that too many of us have reacted so strongly to Barth, for in our zeal to show the deficiencies of his doctrine of Scripture, we have become bibliolaters. (*O Timothy*, Oct. 94).

In Wallace's *The Synoptic Problem*, (available on his website), he supports the redaction approach to the Gospels. This theory teaches that the Gospels were given, not by direct inspiration, but rather by copying from each other, and from a common secondary source. (See *O Timothy*, vol. 15-7, 98). Wallace says:

It is quite impossible to hold that the three synoptic gospels were completely independent from each other. In the least, they had to have shared a common oral tradition (p.1).
We shall see later that before the Gospels were written there did exist a period in which the gospel materials were passed on orally, and it is clear that this oral tradition influenced not only the first of our synoptic Gospels but the subsequent ones as well (p. 4).
The majority of NT scholars hold to Markan priority...This is the view adopted in this paper as well (p.6).
One argument concerning Mark's harder readings...is the probability that neither Luke nor Matthew had pristine copies of Mark at their disposal...An intermediate scribe is probably responsible - either intentionally or unintentionally - or more than a few of the changes which ended up in Luke and Matthew (note 49).

This is characteristic of the kind of scholarship that produces and backs the modern versions. When the Standard Bible and Text are rejected and when verbal preservation is abandoned, a denial or weakening of verbal inspiration will soon follow.

CHAPTER 20

The Great Contrast

We can do no better in closing than to note again *The Translators to the Readers.*

The contrast with what we have just seen above could not be greater.

> Translation it is that openeth the window, to let in the light; that breaketh the shell, that we may eat the kernel; that putteth aside the curtain, that we may look into the most holy place; that removeth the cover of the well, that we may come by the water; even as Jacob rolled away the stone from the mouth of the well, by which means the flocks of Laban were watered. (VI:8,9).

> And in what sort did these assemble? In the trust of their own knowledge, or of their sharpness of wit, or deepness of judgment, as it were in an arm of flesh? At no hand. They trusted in him that hath the key of David, opening, and no man shutting; they prayed to the Lord, the Father of our Lord, to the effect that St Augustine did; O let thy Scriptures be my pure delight; let me not be deceived in them, neither let me deceive by them. In this confidence, and with this devotion, did they assemble together; not too many, lest one should trouble another; and yet many, lest many things haply might escape them. If you ask what they had before them, truly it was the *Hebrew* text of the Old Testament, the *Greek* of the New. These are the two golden pipes, or rather conduits, where through the olive branches empty themselves into the gold. (XV:7-11).

> Neither did we think much to consult the translators or commentators, *Chaldee, Hebrew, Syrian, Greek,* or *Latin,* no, nor the *Spanish, French, Italian,* or *Dutch;* neither did we disdain to revise that which we had done, and to bring back to the anvil that which we had hammered: but having and using as great helps as were needful, and fearing no reproach for slowness, nor coveting praise for expedition, we

have at the length, through the good hand of the Lord upon us, brought the work to that pass that you see. (XV:19-21).

Many other things we might give thee warning of, gentle reader, if we had not exceeded the measure of a Preface already. It remaineth that we commend thee to God, and to the Spirit of His grace, which is able to build further than we can ask or think. He removeth the scales from our eyes, the vail from our hearts, opening our wits that we may understand His Word, enlarging our hearts, yea, correcting our affections, that we may love it above gold and silver, yea, that we may love it to the end. Ye are brought unto fountains of living water which ye digged not; do not cast earth into them, with the Philistines, neither prefer broken pits before them, with the wicked Jews. Others have laboured, and you may enter into their labours. O receive not so great things in vain; O despise not so great salvation! Be not like swine to tread under foot so precious things, neither yet like dogs to tear and abuse holy things. Say not to our Saviour with the *Gergesites*, Depart out of our coasts; neither yet with *Esau* sell your birthright for a mess of pottage. If light be come into the world, love not darkness more than light; if food, if clothing, be offered, go not naked, starve not yourselves.......(XVIII:1-9).

Jack Moorman
London, England
2009

INDEX

Breinigsville, PA USA
22 January 2010
231182BV00005B/2/P